STOVE

chen Maid's Story

OVER A HOT STOVE

A Kitchen Maid's Story

FLO WADLOW

With additional notes by Alan Childs

Allison & Busby Limited
12 Fitzroy Mews
London W1T 6DW
www.allisonandbusby.com

First published in Great Britain in 2007.
This paperback edition published by Allison & Busby in 2013.

A CIP catalogue record for this book is available from
the British Library.

First Edition

ISBN 978-0-7490-1571-8

Typeset in 11.5/19.5 pt Sabon by
Allison & Busby Ltd.

The paper used for this Allison & Busby publication
has been produced from trees that have been legally sourced
from well-managed and credibly certified forests.

Printed and bound by
CPI Group (UK) Ltd, Croydon, CR0 4YY

This book is dedicated with love
to my late husband, Bob,
and to all my family

A lovely portrait of Flo in the late 1930s,
probably aged about twenty-five

INTRODUCTION

by Alan Childs

Flo Wadlow was an amazing lady by any standards, and something of a Norfolk legend in her own lifetime. Her career in full-time domestic service was mainly in the 1930s, and the life she so vividly recalled now seems to us as some distant period of history, so markedly did things change after the Second World War. Flo regarded it as a wonderful opportunity to live in beautiful surroundings, employed by people who, in some cases, were at the very centre of world affairs. By her contact with and proximity to them, Flo felt 'elevated' herself. She would not hear a bad word spoken against the families whose paths crossed with hers whilst in domestic service. Where there were restrictions on what she was allowed to do, she saw these as part of her employers' caring role, especially for the young girls in their charge. It is an experience she would not have missed, despite the hardness of the work, the long hours for little pay, and the often spartan accommodation.

She started as a kitchen maid and ended this part of her life as cook at Blickling Hall no less, just before the Second World War – at the amazingly young age of twenty-three. In a sense, these jobs carried on throughout her long life because she continued to put her culinary skills to good use, whether for intimate dinner parties or large village or county events. Her enjoyment of this job, the vocation of serving up delicious food, carried her through. She was never happier than when her hands were engaged in cooking up masterpieces for people's delight. Her five decades in the village of Heydon, which she loved, were intertwined with many members of the Bulwer (Bulwer-Long) family, descendants of the Bulwers of Heydon Hall, who over the years adopted Flo as their favourite cook – and friend.

Amazingly, her needlework and sewing talents virtually matched her cooking expertise, and her life could so easily have gone in that direction instead. Many local weddings have benefited from Flo's dressmaking skills. She took in her stride the creation of wedding dresses and bridesmaids' dresses, or the 'canvas work' for chairs, or the complex embroidering of hassocks (kneelers) for two of the chapels in St Paul's cathedral. Flo attended the impressive dedication service for the kneelers that she and others had made for the Chapel of the Order of the British Empire.

Music and dressing up to perform on stage were both great interests during her life, as were involvement with the Red Cross, and the WI. Flo also loved driving; distance was never an object for her, nor tackling a long journey alone. Most years she would drive down to Devon to see her brother and his family, and in her eighties she undertook the journey from Norfolk to Alloa in Scotland, on her own, because her sister had been unwell and Flo felt she needed cheering up. About that journey Flo commented: 'I didn't look to see how fast I was going when it was over eighty!'

To visit her cottage was to find, within her hand's reach, a tottering pile of encyclopedias, thesauri and atlases, plus guidebooks to the riches of English buildings. Her thirst for knowledge never ceased, especially her twin loves of history and geography. Her memory was almost infallible, even at later life. To keep her word skills honed she regularly challenged her younger sister to a game of Scrabble. And of course the occasional cake still emerged from her kitchen.

Flo led an active life and was thrilled by the possibility of sharing her memories in print, as she did on numerous occasions in person for local clubs and societies in Norfolk. As might be expected, Flo also took radio and television appearances in her stride. On one occasion, some few years ago, she was one of the stars of the series *Upper Crust* presented by the author and photographer, Christopher Simon Sykes. Flo's role was played out with Sarah Bulwer-Long in her charming kitchen at Heydon Hall, cooking the chicken dish Flo had prepared for a visit of Queen Mary to Blickling Hall, way back in 1938.

It has been a pleasure getting to know Flo Wadlow over these last years and to be able to help with her book. In the course of preparing it, my wife and I have met some delightful people and have gone along intriguing avenues of research. We have visited a number of the houses in the story, and in one, for example, discovered unexpectedly that Elgar and Richard Strauss and Paderewski were all close friends of Flo's employers. These musicians could just possibly have created the music that drifted up to the attics of the house and lulled the young kitchen maid to sleep.

It is essentially Flo's story, in her own words, and one that I have no doubt will give great pleasure to all who read it.

Flo with her mother and baby brother Tom

CHAPTER ONE

Early Life – Holkham

Flo Wadlow was born on 8th December 1912, at Upton Park, in the Borough of West Ham. Her mother Georgina was a cook and her father Thomas Copeland was a porter at Billingsgate Market. When the First World War started on 28th July 1914, her father, who had been a regular soldier in South Africa, was called up as a reserve. He joined the Royal West Kent Regiment. Sadly, during the following year, he was killed. It was just after his death that Flo's brother Tom was born. During those early wartime years, the children were looked after by their grandmother, while their mother went to work in a munitions factory. Flo's first visit to Norfolk, aged about seven, was a memorable event.

We first came to Norfolk on the train, before we even moved here. We came to have a holiday first of all, coming to Liverpool Street from Forest Gate. On the station there was a troop of servicemen all dressed in their uniforms, all lined up. Another guard of honour came and brought the coffin of Edith Cavell and put it on the train. There was a whole carriage for her coffin to be put into and it was all draped with the union flag. It's a scene that has stuck in my mind, and I can see it now. Such a wonderful thing about this lady who was shot by the Germans because she helped our servicemen. And they paid tribute to her. We had to change trains at Wymondham, to go to Wells, so I never saw the reception she got at Norwich – but I did see the sending off in London.

It was the chance friendship of a girl who worked with Flo's mother that led to an invitation to stay with them when the war was over. They stayed in Wells-next-the-Sea, and Flo's family so enjoyed it they decided to move to Wells to live. And by a kind of fate, her mother met and married her young friend's brother, so Flo had a new stepfather. From their marriage three more daughters were to be born, Phyllis, Freda (Alfreda) and Betty. For a time her family lived in one of the cottages at the entrance to Holkham Park.

Holkham Park

I had a very happy childhood at Wells. We also lived at Holkham for a time and mother used to be a cook for the gardeners in the 'Bothy' [small cottage for workmen] there. I loved living at Holkham. We were like 'The Children of the New Forest'. It was really wonderful, and once or twice I had the privilege of going up to the Hall.

As a child, trees always fascinated me and I used to like walking in the woods at Holkham. I found out where there were violets and primroses which I could gather to take home to my mum. I also found out where there was watercress in the streams and there were blackberries too in the woods. I can't really describe the thrill I had – that we could just wander about at will and nobody minded. We seemed to be quite safe, not like today. I spent hours in the park. There was a herd of deer there too, and they used to come right up to the house and rattle their horns in the window. It was an idyllic place for a child to live.

My mother would send me to buy dripping from the Hall cook, but there were other children from the village, from big families, who were allowed to go up to the Hall kitchen, and they were given all sorts of things – stews, or soup or puddings that had been left. They used to take small milk cans to bring their food home in. Once or twice I bribed them to let me go with them, because I wanted to see inside Holkham Hall. I thought it was absolutely fabulous. I thought the saucepans were all made of gold! Of course it was brass really, and copper.

I would have loved to have gone to Holkham to work, but there never seemed to be a place – not when I was ready to leave a job, and I never did get there. In those days all the village people worked on the estate or would do something for the estate, except, for example, the schoolteacher or the pub landlord. It all seemed like one big family. I think I did find that with a lot of places I went to. The families did care about the village people. They were concerned and looked after them.

At Holkham there was a chapel, and now and again they used to have a service in there and all the village could go. So of course we used to troop into the Marble Hall. As a child, I had never seen anything like it before. I thought it was wonderful. Lady Leicester was a very aristocratic lady but she used to think a lot about the village people. She used to go round to see them, to see if they were all right. She used to run the WI, and of course nearly all the ladies of the village had to go, because her Ladyship ran it. They had it after school and I used to go and see what they were up to. I remember once they had a competition where you had to 'Sing, Say or Pay'.

Of course mother had not got a lot of money so she didn't really want to pay, and she *could* sing, but she didn't want to. Her Ladyship said, 'Tell us something that your clever little girl has been doing.' Well I did have a swollen head indeed. Lady Leicester was a nice lady but mother used to get a bit fed up with her because she nearly always used to come in when we were having our tea.

'Oh, you have far more to eat for your tea than I do,' she would say. Of course we did, because that was our main meal and she'd have her dinner afterwards, wouldn't she?

At school we had to learn things more or less off by heart – like our tables. I think to myself now, when I go to the supermarket, I can add up my things in my head whereas these girls can't. They learn how to use computers instead. I tried very hard at school and joined in everything there was. We had school games and a school play. I loved doing anything like that. I remember doing *The Merchant of Venice*, but I wasn't very happy because I had to be Shylock of all people. I'd much rather have been Portia!

Mum was quite a good cook and a needlewoman, and as a child I always loved to help her. They really were my two main interests. When my father was killed, for several years there was only my brother and I with my mother. We had all her attention, so of course there was a great bond with my mum and I would do anything to help her. I could easily cook the dinner by the time I was about eleven, and make a cake and things like that – a very simple sort of cake, or buns. I used to love doing it for Mum.

My mother had a pension for us two children – even after she got married again – so my stepfather didn't have to keep us two. Mother lost *her* pension, but she had a pension for my brother and me. I think mine was about ten shillings a week. That was quite a bit of money in them days you see. Mother didn't want to lose that, so I stayed at home until I was sixteen.

I used to go and help a lady who lived across the road. She had TB and she used to live in one of them little huts they had out of doors, which turned round to catch the sun. I used to go there and cook the dinner for her and her husband. I would run errands for her, and other people as well, and do all kinds of jobs. And I helped mother with her sewing. The rector of Wells, or his daughter, would bring sewing jobs for my mother to do and I would help her do them. The rector came round one day and asked me what I wanted to do, so I replied that I'd like to sew as well. He said he'd see what he could do. He went to Norwich where there was a big shop called Chamberlins, which was just near the Guildhall. He went there because they used to have apprentice dressmakers. But when we heard that my mother would have to pay for me to go, well that put a different complexion on it altogether. We couldn't possibly afford that, so I thought I'd turn to my other liking and I would learn to be a cook.

The rector told me about the agency in Norwich where you put your name down for a job, and he gave me a reference. Before I ever went into service he said, 'You don't really want to go anywhere where there are young children. Let me warn you – nannies, oh, are terrible people, and ever so particular! You will find, if you ever go where there is a nanny, they are worse than the lady and gentleman are – so fussy and everything.' I don't think I ever went where there was a nanny. Well, the only place where they had nannies was Hatfield and that was for their grandchildren, and I didn't come in contact with the nanny either, not there.

I told my mother I didn't want to be a 'maid-of-all-work'. I just wanted to work in the kitchen. I didn't want to do housework. It never interested me one little bit – and it still doesn't, to tell you the truth. And of course I couldn't earn as much as the pension. If I had gone as a maid at the rectory I'd have earned five shillings a week.

I thought I would go to London and make my fortune. If you were in Norfolk you had about twelve pounds a year where in London you got twenty pounds. Eight pounds' difference was a lot. I put my name down at this agency in Prince of Wales Road, in Norwich. I had heard that people in London were very keen to have Norfolk girls because they were nearly always quite healthy and strong, and not afraid of hard work. So I stood a good chance you see, although quite truthfully, I wasn't Norfolk at all. But I didn't tell them that!

Entrance to 78 Onslow Gardens in South Kensington.
'Those blooming steps were the bane of my life.'

CHAPTER TWO

South Kensington and Shenley

Aged sixteen, young Flo set out for the big city, missing her mother of course, but excited at her new life. This first job was working for a retired army officer in South Kensington. She was never quite sure what her mother felt about her ambition to be a cook, even though she had herself cooked for a time at Holkham.

My mother appreciated what I wanted to do but I don't really know if she was pleased or not. She never did say. My grandmother *wasn't* pleased. She couldn't understand my mum letting me go into service. I said, 'Well Mum didn't make me go at all. It was my choice.' She'd never heard anything so ridiculous. A girl should do what she's told. I should have gone in a shop or something. Well I wouldn't have had half the interest in life I've had if I'd gone into a shop, of course I wouldn't. But Mum *was* quite proud of me really! Of course I got terribly homesick, but the days were full of work.

My grandmother lived in East Ham, and I thought that if I went to London to work, I could go to see my granny sometimes – not realising how far South Kensington was from East Ham. You used to have to go on the Underground. Even out of my London wages I couldn't afford many tickets, but I know I went there once.

I went off to London as bold as anything and got myself on the Underground to South Kensington. It must have been January 1929 when I went there because it was just after Christmas, after I was sixteen. They told me to have a taxi from the station, but when I asked the taxi man to take me to Onslow Gardens he said, 'It's just round the corner,' and so of course I walked to where I had to go.

I arrived at 78 Onslow Gardens, the home of Colonel Young. He wasn't a married gentleman and his two sisters who lived with him weren't married either. The day after I got there, the parlour maid took me upstairs to be introduced to the elder of the ladies. She had waived the idea of me going through an interview. Mostly they interviewed their girls before they employed them but as she had had such a good reference for me from Norfolk, and that was a long way to come, they waived that aside. But she did want to meet me and talk to me and see what kind of person I was. After that of course I never saw them! You didn't – not in the kitchen. That was the only thing I thought was a bit sad really, because we never did see the people who we worked for.

The parlour maid's name was Florence so of course I couldn't be called Florence too. They asked me what my second name was, and when I said 'Georgina' – well I couldn't be called Georgina. That was far too big a mouthful, and too smart really, for just a kitchen maid. So they called me 'Ena' and that took a bit of getting used to.

Luckily I had a little bedroom to myself, right on the very top floor. Most of these houses were about four or five storeys high. The bedrooms were unheated and the room was very bare – an iron bedstead, a chest of drawers and a chair, that was my lot. I had a curtain and a rail in one corner where I could hang my Sunday best. Fortunately I hadn't got a lot of clothes so it didn't really matter. I didn't want a wardrobe. It was very basic there, but things did improve as I went along. My mother had bought me an 'alarum' clock because I had to be downstairs in the kitchen, ready to work, at half past six in the morning. I don't think I had been up at half past six before in my life, so I took my alarum clock with me and the first night I was there I could hardly go to sleep for having the clock ticking. You see I wasn't used to having a clock. I put it in the drawer, then I couldn't hear it, and I thought I shouldn't wake up when the alarm went. So I had to have it, and I didn't get much sleep at all.

There was the cook [cum housekeeper] and myself in the kitchen. There was a parlour maid and a housemaid and they had a girl who worked between them – a 'between maid' ['tweeny']. She would help the housemaid first thing in the morning, and at lunchtime she would change her dress and have a black frock and a little apron, and she would have to go and help the parlour maid wait on the people. She would help wash up in the pantry because they washed up all the silver there. I didn't have to do the silver or the glass or anything like that. I had all the pots and pans to do and I did have the plates to wash up. The china plates of course that they had in the dining room, they were very particular about them. You washed them up with soft soap that you whisked up in the water. You had to have another enamel bowl in one of them big stone sinks with some plain hot water, which you had to rinse them all in, then put them in the rack. You weren't really allowed to wipe them up. The cook said there were more germs on a tea cloth than there was on anything.

I remembered my mother's words: 'You mustn't think that you know what to do. If you're not sure, you ask the cook how she likes it done.' And I think the poor cook must have thought I was a complete ignoramus because nearly everything I asked her how she liked it done, so that I got it right!

They talk about hygiene in a kitchen nowadays but

they don't know a thing, compared to the old cook in that house. My life revolved more or less around cleaning everywhere. The kitchen was scrubbed from top to bottom every now and again. You had to have the sweep every four months I think, on account of the kitchen ranges. I suppose it was really to do with the insurance. There was a wall plate in the basement at the back of the ranges. He would take it off and sweep from there. The cook then thought everything was covered in soot, even in the kitchen, so everything was scrubbed from top to bottom. Every day the kitchen tables would be scrubbed a couple of times, after lunch and after dinner at night – even the legs of the table. The dresser, where all the copper pots and pans were on, that was scrubbed down. People haven't got any idea nowadays. Once over with Flash and that's your lot. We didn't have many chairs, only about two. They were whitewood, and scrubbed all down. The kitchen doors were also, and the cupboards were all scrubbed out. I have never seen so much scrubbing in my life as I did at that first place. The cook was ever so particular and ever so fussy. You had to have a hessian apron to do your scrubbing in. I wish I'd had a photograph of myself. Whatever I looked like I can't think!

For the first week, I think, the cook used to come down with me and help me to light the stove. We had a big kitchen range – a monstrosity of a thing which had to be black-leaded. There was a rack over the top and lots of handles, knobs and things on the cooker which were like steel – that all had to be rubbed down with emery paper every day. All had to shine as though it was varnished. I had to clean the flues out every so often, and woe betide me if I didn't. The cook knew the next minute if I hadn't done them. That did take a lot of getting used to, lighting the kitchen fire and getting the kettle boiling, because we hadn't any gas stoves or electric stoves, or anything like that – just this cooker, and that heated the water as well. Normally Cook would come down about seven and she'd make the tea, and then we'd go about our work.

My next morning job was to polish the doorknob and the letterbox on the front door, and then I had to clean the front doorsteps as well. They had to be whitened with a kind of hearthstone. Those blooming steps, they were the bane of my life. If it was a wet day, and if the postman came after I'd done them, there would be his footmarks all over them, and of course they had to be done again. If there was anybody particular coming for lunch or afternoon tea, you couldn't have dirty steps, so of course they had to be done again. Sometimes the ladies would have an 'at-home' day and have people in for cucumber sandwiches and fairy cakes. The steps would have to be whitened again, so you see it was more or less a regular job. In those days too we used to have quite a lot of fogs in London, and of course fog is one of the worst things for brass doorknobs, so they often had to be done more than once a day, even without visitors. Everyone was so particular and things were much more labour-intensive.

Another job I had to do before breakfast was to clean the colonel's boots, and then I helped to get the breakfast. I had to set the breakfast in the servants' hall for us, and when we'd had that I would go upstairs and make my bed and tidy my room. Then I'd come down and help Cook with whatever she had to do – like prepare the vegetables and help cook the servants' meals. I'd helped my mother quite a bit so I knew quite a lot of different vegetables, but even so they had some which I had never heard of before, like artichokes. One thing that has always stayed in my mind that the cook told me about vegetables: 'The vegetables that grow in the ground you cook in the pot with the lid on, and you always put them in cold water. Vegetables that grow on top of the ground, like peas, beans and cabbage, you put in boiling water and you don't put the lid on.' But of course nowadays we do put lids on, and we don't cook vegetables half as long as we used to then. You used to cook cabbage for about twenty minutes in those days, but now it's in and out of the pan in no time at all.

There would be other things to help the cook with too, and I'd lay the table ready for her. She had her board, and she would have knives, forks and spoons all ready, and basins and perhaps some spare plates. She would have a few vegetables, like onions and carrots, in case she wanted to make soup. And on the table there would be little canisters, one with flour and another with caster sugar, and there was salt and pepper. Everything was all laid out – you had to have it all ready. You might have other ideas because she used to write the menus out in a book that was in a glass case. You looked at the menu and you could see what she was going to need, and more or less what she was going to prepare. You had to see she had the saucepans ready to hand. She didn't want to climb up on the dresser.

And there was the washing-up to do afterwards, and you couldn't put things in a dishwasher! No electric kettles, no electric mixers, nothing.

The food was a bit spartan this first job I had, but I think that was because it was in London. They hadn't got a garden or anything like that, or fruit growing. There, we had so much butter a week – about a couple of ounces. The cook kept really very strict control, for example over how much sugar was used. We had enough food but not overdone. I had my meals in the servants' hall. It was the only place I ever did. Normally the kitchen staff were just too busy with the servants' and dining-room lunches and had to take their own lunch in the kitchen, when they could. In the servants' hall, being a young girl, I wasn't allowed to speak unless I was spoken to. I suppose they must have asked me all different sorts of things. I told them I used to help Mum do the sewing for the rectory and all that.

There was no time off in the afternoon in that London house. If there was any time to spare I would have to help to do sewing, darning or whatever. I would help the housemaids and the parlour maid mend serviettes. You had to darn them carefully. There the cook would find you a job, even if it was tidying the drawers up or something like that. And you'd only got to move a drawer and it'd be untidy again. But the cook where I went was a kind soul and she looked after me well.

I had a half-day off a week and one Sunday afternoon every fortnight. I had to learn to do things when the cook had her half-day. I could get their dinner in the dining room, at night-time, but of course she would make what they had. People seemed to have ever so many courses years ago – sometimes soup, sometimes fish and meat and a pudding and sometimes a savoury. The soup I would only have to heat up. If it was a thick soup I would probably just have to do some vegetables or macaroni – just to pop in at the last minute. She would leave everything ready for me to warm up, so that I hadn't got a lot to do when she was out. So I really got a fair knowledge of cooking in that job.

When it was *my* Sunday off I used to go to the Methodist church – sometimes to the Kingsway Hall and sometimes to the Central Hall in Westminster. The parlour maid asked me one Sunday if I would like to go with her to the Central Hall. I nearly always used to go with the parlour maid – so she knew how much I loved the music. But I also loved going there because in the afternoon there'd be a girls' meeting, and you could have your tea there – one of those nice sticky buns with a cup of tea. And there they used to have a proper choir concert, at six o'clock. They had a soprano, a contralto, a tenor and a bass – they all sung their solos. I thoroughly enjoyed the music. Then at half past six we'd have the evening service. After that we'd come home. Sometimes in the week I used to go to a meeting there and I often went to Hyde Park and saw Lord Soper [a prominent Methodist minister].

There were concerts in London for charity, and ladies would buy tickets. If they didn't want them for themselves, they would probably give them to the staff. The ladies in church often used to buy tickets for special causes and they evidently bought some tickets for *Messiah* at the Albert Hall. They had been before, and they didn't want to go again, so they asked the parlour maid if she would like to go, and said she could take somebody with her. She asked me if I'd like to go. Would I like to go to the Albert Hall! Absolutely fantastic. I can picture it now, even though it was over seventy years ago.

There was the London Philharmonic Orchestra and a great choir, as well as the soloists singing all the main parts, and of course the Albert Hall was filled with people. I shall never forget Dr Malcolm Sargent all my life. He wasn't made a 'Sir' then, when I saw him. I was wafted away on cloud nine. I've never forgotten the thrill of it. I wasn't a kitchen maid at all on that night.

* * *

I loved going to Kensington Gardens and to all the shops in Kensington High Street – Pontings, and Derry & Toms. I'd walk across Hyde Park and go to Selfridges. Even if I didn't buy anything, I might go and have a look round and try on a few hats! Sometimes at the beginning of the month I might even go to the pictures. I generally had some money for the first week and then the next three weeks I didn't have any! It didn't last very long in those days.

The cook said to me one day that I hadn't told her that this girls' club I'd joined was going on an outing. I said that they were going on a Saturday, and I didn't have a Saturday off. She said that if I had asked her, she could perhaps have arranged it, but I told her that I didn't like to ask because I couldn't really afford to go. Anyway she paid for me to go and we went to Buckinghamshire, near Princes Risborough, where there are some lovely woods. While we were out in one of the villages they were selling flowers at a cottage gate, and I thought I'd buy the cook a bunch of flowers. Well I couldn't have given her anything better. If I had knighted her she couldn't have been more pleased! She was absolutely thrilled to think I had thought of her.

Just over the year I thought I'd make a change, because you can get in a rut. They'd have a joint on Sunday, cold on Monday and have it done up on Tuesday. Perhaps some chops on Wednesday – and you got into the same routine. You just cooked what they liked. You had to stay a year because they paid for your fare, but if you didn't stay, you had to forfeit that. In the summer the family went away for a fortnight so we could have a fortnight off. Having about thirty shillings for my month's wages, if I paid my fare home, which was nearly a pound, and giving my mother ten shillings for my keep, I wouldn't have anything for myself. Then just before the family went away, the colonel sent down an envelope, and in it was a pound for cleaning his boots – so I was saved again. I went to the agency and got a job in the village of Shenley, in Hertfordshire, quite near Elstree. The house was called 'Ridgehurst'.

Ridgehurst House

There were two elderly people, the lady and gentleman, and they were German people – naturalised British with German origins – and they were ever such musical people. They used to go to London quite a lot to different concerts. That was a lovely house and beautiful gardens in this little village. And on the end of the house they had a lovely big conservatory or music room, with windows all round. They used to have all their friends come and they used to play music. They'd perhaps have a dinner party first and then they'd play.

Flo was working for Edward Speyer, a wealthy banker and cousin of Sir Edgar Speyer. Edward was a great friend of Brahms, but also, like his cousin, a friend of Sir Edward Elgar. The composer stayed regularly at Ridgehurst and during one visit, in July 1919, to appease his host's annoyance with smoking in the house, Elgar wrote a forty-two-second (!) 'Smoking Cantata'. Another famous visitor to this house where Flo worked was the pianist and composer Paderewski. When Sir Edgar Speyer brought Richard Strauss over to England to conduct Ein Heldenleben, *Strauss also visited Ridgehurst. The music room was by all accounts very special, thirty-six feet by twenty-seven feet with a raised platform, panelling and a moulded plaster ceiling.*

Supporting the musical life of the house 'below stairs', Flo was aware that the number of staff was just a little more generous. The work and the chores continued as before.

We had a butler there and he had a boy who he was training up to be a footman. There were two housemaids and there were two maids in the kitchen, so it was just getting a little bit of a bigger establishment. I was climbing up the ladder a little bit. There I did the same kinds of things – I helped Cook with the vegetables – but I didn't have any front doorsteps to clean. No knocker, and no boots either! I didn't have quite so much scrubbing except in the kitchen still, and there was the kitchen range to do.

But I was working entirely in the kitchen, cooking the servants' meals, and helping to cook the vegetables for the dining room. And I began to learn a bit or two of French because they had all their menus written in French. I would have to know what kind of garnish they would want with different things, like with 'Consommé Royale' you would have to make a little egg custard and cut it all up into different shapes to pop in; with 'Consommé Italienne' there were little bits of spaghetti chopped up.

And there too of course they had a garden and gardeners, whereas in London they hadn't a garden. They had most peculiar vegetables: kohlrabi [like a swollen radish growing above the ground] and cardoons [like giant sticks of celery, up to six feet high], salsify [also called 'goat's beard', with an oyster-like flavour when the roots were boiled], and scorzonera [similar to horseradish]. They used to grow these things years ago but they have gone out of fashion now. They weren't much to write home about anyhow. I'd much rather have beans and peas and celery and things like that.

Nowadays you have vegetables all the year round but in those days you didn't. Vegetables and fruit weren't transported into the country like they are now, so they grew things in their own kitchen gardens. You had a season for different things.

We were in the country too, living near Shenley. There was a bus from there where you could go to Radlett and other places, and you could go to the pictures when it was your day off. I don't think I went much further afield than that. I got friendly with some people in the village because I thought I would go to the WI. My mum belonged to the WI you will remember. I joined not because of the talks or anything but because they had a tennis club and their own tennis court and I liked to play tennis.

Flo did not find Christmas at all special in service –
partly because of the present of hideous black stockings
that usually came her way. Her Christmas in Shenley,
however, was memorable for cooking some dreadful
venison from the Black Forest.

I always shudder when I think of it. I never really
remember Christmas in any of the jobs I've been in,
except that mostly you had a pair of black stockings
for your Christmas present. We *always* had to wear
black shoes and stockings. I swore I'd never wear
them again, not in my life! They're very fashionable
now, but of course they look a lot different to the ones
I had to wear, I can assure you. We didn't have nylons
in those days – they were either wool or lisle. Terrible
things!

I have always thought that venison must have been
buried in the Black Forest, for how long I don't know,
because I never smelt anything like it in all my life. It
smelt rotten. I couldn't eat anything on that day. I felt
really sick and the smell must have gone all through
the house – it was awful.

But Flo's lasting memory of working for the Speyers was that it was a house of music. Flo loved it for that, although sadly she was unaware of just who might have been playing the music that she fell asleep to!

I remember the big music room and the house parties where musical guests brought their instruments to play. I often went to sleep to the sound of music drifting up to the top of the house. From my bedroom I could hear them playing long into the night.

Flo aged eighteen, in her uniform as kitchen maid at Mapleton near Edenbridge, Kent. Servants were usually expected to provide their own uniforms.

CHAPTER THREE

Edenbridge and Hilgay

Once again, Flo stayed about a year then thought she would move on to gain more experience. Her next appointment was to a house called 'Mapleton', between Edenbridge and Westerham, in Kent. This time her employers were younger people. And she was now earning the princely sum of thirty pounds a year.

Mapleton House, from a painting by Samuel Henry
Faudel-Phillips, the owner in late-Victorian times.

That was a lovely part of the country and they had lovely grounds on the estate, and there was a cricket pitch out at the back of the house and a pavilion, beyond the kitchen garden. Mr and Mrs Pilbrow were such nice people – very kind. The gentleman used to go to London every day on business. He worked in the City, near St Paul's Churchyard. The chauffeur used to take him to the station at Westerham and he would pick him up at night. We would wait for the car to come and knew that within about half an hour he had had a drink and had his bath and changed, and that it would be dinner time. They had a son, Ashley, who was at Cambridge and they had a younger son of about seven. He had a tutor who came in, in the mornings, to get him ready for preparatory school.

They were fanatical about cricket and they had their own cricket team – mostly the people who worked on the estate. The butler, Mr Brickett, was the captain of the team and the chauffeurs and the gardeners were in it. Mr Pilbrow played, and Master Ashley when he was down from Cambridge. They used to have teams come from various parts of Kent, from the village, and other villages round. I suppose they were in some kind of league. We had quite a lot of teams come then and sometimes they used to go away and play.

This was a cricketing household, with a team made up of members of staff. The butler, Mr Brickett, is wearing the striped blazer.

We had marvellous cricket teas for them – bread rolls and sausage rolls, meat pies and sandwiches and cakes of all kinds. They had a real spread, I can assure you. They also had a big dinner for the cricket team, though we didn't cater for that.

That was held in the village hall of Four Elms, near Edenbridge. All the team went to the dinner, but we were allowed to go afterwards, when they had the dances. I had never been to a dance before. Of course I didn't dare tell my mother I was going to a dance because, I mean, what wicked things you could have got up to at a dance. I was quite excited about that. The village boys and some of the young lads who followed the cricket team were very friendly – and quite interested in the girls who worked at the big house! So they taught me how to dance. I had a whale of a time – thoroughly enjoyed myself.

You were allowed too to go to dances in the village but you see, you weren't allowed to have young men – to bring you home. No followers! The under chauffeur had to bring one of the cars – not the best limousine, but the one used for shopping. I think he used to dance himself, if I remember. Mr and Mrs Pilbrow were very caring about their staff. The under chauffeur took us all to the dance and brought us home. No hanky-panky!

I don't think you would have been dismissed if

you had a boyfriend, but they liked to look after me how my mother would have done. They were responsible for you, weren't they? Well, that's how I felt. It was a terrible thing in those days if a girl got into trouble so I think it was really more about them looking after you. I could have had a boyfriend easily because the village boys were ever so friendly.

The butler, and in that case the housekeeper, Mrs Brickett, his wife, were the ones who were strict. They probably had orders from the ladies and gentlemen, but *they* were the ones I knew. Often such people were the reason some young girls didn't like being in service. They got with the wrong people and didn't like it – hated every minute of it. I was very fortunate, or perhaps I looked at it in a different way to some people. I felt they were really only trying to look after me. That's how my mother had impressed it on me – to be a good girl and do what I was told.

At Mapleton I did learn quite a bit of cooking. The butler's wife, Mrs Brickett, even if strict, was a nice lady. She had been the cook previously but she had been ill. She couldn't do the cooking so they got a young cook, and I was the kitchen maid. We had the butler and the parlour maid and two housemaids again.

When Cook went on her whole day off, Mrs Brickett would come in to help. She came into the kitchen and she showed me lots of things. She taught me how to make bread. The first loaf of bread I made I think was the best I ever did! I learnt all different kinds of pastry – short-crust, choux pastry and puff pastry too. It seemed miraculous how that should rise; and all the little leaves to make vol-au-vents. I learnt different kinds of sauces like mayonnaise and Hollandaise. Every drop of oil we had to stir with a wooden spoon in those days. She taught me how to make soufflés – hot and cold – and different kinds of meat dishes.

She was ever so good to me, and I was eager to learn. I suppose it was nice for her as well to be able to teach someone who appreciated her. She really laid the basis of my knowledge of cooking. I learnt things like how to make a Genoese sponge cake and we used to make the liver pâté. She was very good, and she

58

did teach me quite a lot of things I hadn't ever done before, or learnt at home.

Preparing the food would depend upon what kinds of vegetables you were going to need. If you were having spinach, for example, we would cook the spinach and it would all go through a sieve, and perhaps then you would make a sauce and add the spinach to it at night. You might do the potatoes in the morning. You might cut them up how they wanted them done. If you were having 'Duchess' potatoes you would mash them in the morning and mix the egg with them and pipe them out – or make little crêpes and all that kind of thing, in the morning.

Generally they had soup and fish, and meat and sweet. Sometimes they might not have the fish as well, but often they did have the four courses. If they had a dinner party, they would have five or six. A lot of things were prepared in the morning – like the pudding would probably be prepared in the morning. Tarts they would usually have for lunch. Soufflés and soup would be prepared in the morning. If it was going to be a thick soup that would have to be put through the hair sieve [like a coarse muslin]. There was masses of work really to be done. I still had to do the kitchen table and the kitchen floor and all that every day, the scullery floor and all the washing up, but there weren't all the passages to clean. The house was all on one level. We weren't in the basement – downstairs, like I had been before – so it was much nicer there.

To help Flo explore the Kent countryside she decided to invest in a bicycle.

Well you could buy a bicycle for about two pounds in those days – not two hundred pounds like you pay nowadays. On my day off I sometimes used to cycle to Tunbridge Wells to see a friend of mine, Dorothy, who I went to school with in Wells. She worked in Tunbridge Wells. Sometimes I would go on a bus. Dorothy did find a young man and she settled down and lived down that way. So if I'd stayed there longer I think I could have done the same. Fate takes a hand sometimes, doesn't it?

You could go on the Green-Line Bus from

Westerham, and you could go to London. If you wanted to go on the bus the under chauffeur was allowed to take you to the bus stop and to pick you up again at night. The butler would arrange all the details and times.

In Kent we lived next door to where Winston Churchill lived. I saw that great man, one day, when I had my half-day. I saw him building his wall at Chartwell. There was a public right of way that went past his house and he didn't like people looking in his garden, so he built a wall to keep 'em out.

One morning when I went to the bathroom to get washed and clean my teeth before I went downstairs to work, I collapsed. I shared a room with the under parlour maid and she came running to find out what had happened and she found me in a heap on the floor. She went and told Mr and Mrs Brickett. They got the doctor and they found I'd got diphtheria, so I had to go into an isolation hospital. I was the only patient in the whole of Kent, and they had to get two nurses specially from London, one a day nurse and one a night nurse, to look after me. The housekeeper,

Mrs Brickett, used to get the under chauffeur to bring her every day to see me, and she talked to me through the window. She used to send cards to my mum to tell her how I was getting on. Now you wouldn't get that from many people.

One day she asked me, since I would be in hospital six weeks or more, if they should get somebody permanent in my place or somebody temporary until I was better. I thought about it seriously. I had been there a year – year and a half – so I felt I might just as well leave. I said they should get somebody permanently. When it was time for me to go home Mrs Brickett and the under chauffeur, they packed all my things up for me and brought the car to the hospital. My bike was on top of the car. They took me to the station in London and put me on the train and off I went home. I couldn't have been looked after nicer. They were some of the nicest people I ever did come across. When Mrs Brickett came to say goodbye to me she said, 'You will have another job in the kitchen, won't you, because I really think you have the makings of a good cook.'

With the newfound freedom of her bicycle, Flo thought she would get a job back in Norfolk. She would be able to cycle home to see her mother occasionally.

I never realised how big Norfolk was. I got this job at 'Woodhall', Hilgay, which is a long way from Wells. There, apart from half a day once a week and half a day once a fortnight, once a month we had a *whole* day off. And I *did* cycle home to Wells, which was only about forty-eight miles!

Woodhall in Hilgay, north-west Norfolk, is a gracious Tudor house. Its claim to fame was that Captain William Manby lived here. He invented the rocket (or 'mortar') device, used to save shipwrecked crews.

In this house there were two gentlemen: the old gentleman, Mr Stocks, and his son, Captain Eric. There was a butler and a footman and a hall boy and they had a valet for Captain Eric. There were two housemaids and the cook, and I was the kitchen maid. There was a scullery maid there as well. She was a nice girl and I'm friends with her to this day. I did have a lot more cooking to do there. I did all the servants' meals and I even had to get the dogs' dinners ready, because they were 'shooting people' and so the dogs had to have a special menu – special meat and everything cooked for them. Some days for example, if we didn't have cabbage for the dining room or the servants' hall, I had to cook cabbage especially for the dogs. I learnt such a lot there with all the game birds – and different vegetables.

All the meat had to be prepared. At Hilgay, being shooting people, they would have pheasants and partridges and hares – and rabbit for the staff – all that to prepare as well, and cook. You did get more and more experienced! I never was squeamish like Molly, the scullery maid. She made out that she didn't like doing it. She would pluck the pheasants but she didn't like drawing them. I had to do that. I think she got round Cook, so Florence had to do them!

Sometimes you made little quenelles of rabbit or chicken, and the meat was pounded first in a mortar and pestle and then put through a sieve raw, before it was mixed with some sauce and egg, and steamed. There was ages of work putting it through a sieve. That's why you really wanted so many staff, didn't you?

I'll never forget once when we were at Woodhall and we had a big shooting lunch there. We'd made some soup, and the 'guns' were round the house in the garden, and a pheasant came flying right through the kitchen window and landed on the table. I grabbed hold of the bird and opened the window and threw it out. Well of course that was as frightened as anything. Everybody laughed at me, the gardeners and everybody. 'Why didn't you wring its neck, Florence?' Well I never thought about that, and I wouldn't dare wring its neck, poor thing. But there was glass in everything, 'cause it came straight through the window, and we had to strain everything through hair sieves. You can imagine, feathers and glass all about. Well you couldn't give anybody food with glass in, could you? We hadn't got time to prepare everything all again; it was bad enough having to sieve it all.

From Hilgay we went to London, in the 'Season'. They had a lovely place in Cadogan Square, just off the Brompton Road. While I was there I bought myself a sewing machine in the Brompton Road. We used to buy material from Pontings at four and a half pence a yard, and I used to make dresses for me and the scullery maid. We used to go on the train up to London. They had a large kitchen garden at Hilgay, so when we were in London they used to send up a big hamper of vegetables and fruit. They would take it either to Hilgay or Downham Market and put it on the train, and then the chauffeur in London would go to Liverpool Street to pick it up. So we had all fresh vegetables from the estate.

The family did a fair amount of entertaining. They had several big lunch parties in London – we had more lunch parties there than dinner parties.

Even then, though, we used to have soup and fish and meat and savoury. We didn't have sweet very often because there wasn't a Mrs Stocks. It makes you wonder how they ate all that. Mostly the food would be dished on silver dishes, and the footman would come to the kitchen and collect them, and they had a big butler's tray to carry them through to the dining room. The butler and the footman would hand the things round, but of course I never did go in the dining room or even around the house much, because you weren't allowed to go in the parts that weren't 'your own'.

While I was there Mr Stock's niece was presented at Court. Her mother didn't have a London house so they came and stayed at Cadogan Square and she went from there. We were allowed to go up to the drawing room and see this girl in all her finery. What she must have felt like I don't know – us girls looking at her, and examining her dress. She didn't seem to mind.

They had quite a lot of shooting parties in the wintertime at Hilgay. Sometimes they would have their lunch out in a farmhouse at the further end of the estate, and we would probably have to make chicken casseroles, or beef or Irish stew, for the 'guns'. We'd put it all in a haybox. This was like a big wooden box and there was another container you could put into it. You put this middle piece in and packed your hay all round the sides of it – you had to do it very tight – and then you put your casserole in, that was hot from the oven. And then put a lid on and the outer lid on, so it was totally covered with hay, and with a couple of lids. It was to keep the food hot when they were right at the other end of the estate and they didn't have time to get back to the main house for lunch. It wouldn't work if it wasn't packed properly.

We had to provide the lunch for the beaters. They all had a baked potato each, and we cooked perhaps either some boiled bacon or some salt beef, and we would make up some meat sandwiches, with a bottle of beer! Of course the people who were staying in the house would come home and have a big dinner at night-time.

There weren't any fridges, not there. We still had an icebox in the larder, like a chest, all lead-lined, and the fishmonger would bring you a big slab of ice. It was a fairly big chest so I think it would last about two weeks. You would put the ice in the chest and you either put things round, or on top of the ice, depending on how cold you wanted them to keep. Fresh fish and meat would go on the ice and was covered generally either with a tea cloth or a piece of clean blanket. Cooked meat wouldn't matter so much. That was often just put in the larder, not in the ice chest. The larder was mostly down a few steps, or in the cellar, to keep things cool. In the larder they nearly always had a marble slab for coolness – where the cook made her pastry. In the summer there would be butter in the chest, but not so near the ice. You didn't want it frozen hard! The butter we put in a bowl and used to shape it with a couple of butter pats. Some of it you'd flatten, then curl it up.

Probably you had your provisions about once a week, and you would have all sorts of things round the edges of the ice. But it was mainly if the fishmonger had been, and brought you some fish that would probably go on the top to keep until the next day, or the day after that. That's where they got the idea of freezers from! Fish used to come from King's Lynn and they would put it on a train and we would get it at Hilgay or Downham Market, where they arranged for it to come. It would be packed in ice on the train. They would also use some of the ice if they wanted to make ice cream. You would have ice and freezing salt and you had a 'paddle' thing and you had to turn a handle.

It was a happy staff really. Cook was a bit funny at times – a Welsh lady. Sometimes she was a bit temperamental. Sometimes she would be all talk, and be as friendly as anything, where another time she wouldn't talk to you at all. We didn't really know how to take her at times. She had a niece who was working in London, in the kitchen as well. When we went to Cadogan Square her niece would come round to see her aunt and they used to jabber away in Welsh. I thought that was very amusing because you see we didn't know a thing they were talking about. She said that all we girls thought about was boys, dancing and dresses. So I was just the normal sort of girl!

When Flo was able to attend any dances she found herself literally 'one step ahead' of some of the other servants, because she had learnt all the new dances down in Kent. She was now able to impress some of the young men by being 'with it', up with the latest dance craze.

I think the new dances were way ahead for Hilgay. I knew how to do the 'palais glide' and all those kind of things. Well the footman and the hall boy couldn't believe it, so of course we had to teach them how to do it. We thought we were on to a good thing there. Molly borrowed her mother's gramophone and we got some records, and in the servants' hall at night, after supper, we used to teach these boys how to dance. But of course when we went to the dance they picked the village girls, and never looked at us!

I was at Hilgay about two years and thoroughly enjoyed it. I thought it was time again to make a move because I had learnt as much as I thought I could. I went to an agency in London 'cause we were working in London at the time. The butler, Mr Orchard, was a very nice man and as I got the letters from the agency about the different jobs I could have, he advised me which ones I ought to try for.

And when a letter came informing Flo that the Marquess of Salisbury at Hatfield House required the services of a bright young kitchen maid, the butler had no hesitation in encouraging Flo to go for it.

'Oh I should go to Hatfield if I were you – you'll get very good training there.'

The Georgian kitchen at Hatfield occupied two storeys of the
house and was in full use until 1939.

CHAPTER FOUR

Hatfield House

At Hatfield House Flo worked for the 4th Marquess of Salisbury, who had been Aide-de-Camp to both King Edward VII and King George V, and was Lord Privy Seal from 1924 to 1929.

Hatfield House was a different cup of tea altogether. The Marquess of Salisbury and his wife were there. He was an elderly gentleman but he was very active in parliamentary affairs and was Leader of the House of Lords at that time. I went there about the 1st of January 1935. There was the Marquess and his wife the Marchioness, and his brother, Lord Hugh Cecil, lived with them. The Salisburys' son was Viscount Cranborne, and he was very influential in the Conservative Party. He worked with Anthony Eden at the Foreign Office. Hatfield seemed to me like a step up the ladder. I'd worked for very nice people, and they were all gentry – but to work for a marquess, I'd never encountered them before. I felt elevated as well!

Modern Flo in front of Hatfield House

Sometimes during the week we would go to Arlington Street – their London house – when his Lordship was in the House of Lords or if anything was going on up there, or if they were entertaining anybody. Sometimes there would only be the head kitchen maid who went and we would be left in the country. When we went to 21 Arlington Street, there was a resident housekeeper, and there would be a girl in the scullery there. She was a little girl whose father was an out-of-work Welsh miner at the time. Arlington Street was just off Piccadilly, by the corner of The Ritz, so I was right in the heart of London.

The family also had an estate at Cranborne in Dorset, where they got their other title from, and we used to go and stay down there too, in the summer time. For this we had special transport for the staff – one of those charabancs, the very old type of bus. One of the chauffeurs would drive us, either up to London or down to Cranborne. There was a housekeeper at the London house who was always there and there was a housekeeper at Hatfield who was always here. There were one or two staff in London all the time, but mostly when his Lordship was in the House of Lords we would go up there.

We had a much greater staff at Hatfield. There were lots of rooms right up in the top of the house. In some places where I've been, the butler would live out of doors, but most of them lived in here. The chauffeurs lived out but the footmen all lived in. Her Ladyship had a lady's maid and there was a valet for his Lordship and a valet for Lord Hugh Cecil. The butler was called the steward there, and we had to call him 'sir'! The butler's pantry was where they kept all the silver, and where the silver was cleaned. The third footman, Edward, would clean that. The first footman would be more responsible for answering the door, and answering the telephone, but they used to take it in turns. At Hatfield, Charles was the first footman and Stanley was the second. Stanley was a nice young man – I liked him. Charles was a bit haughty. He was a very good-looking boy – and he knew it! He had his nose up in the air. He thought he was the cat's whiskers – God's gift to women. If he could find fault with anything he did. One time Charles wasn't well. He had a touch of gastritis, so he had to go on a diet. Mrs Harris, the cook, was up in arms, having to cook special food for him – fish and all that. 'Oh,' I said, 'Nothing gives me better delight. I'm glad he can't eat what the others have. He's got to have fish done in water. It serves him jolly well right.' He eventually went with Lord Tweedsmuir [the author

John Buchan] when he went as Governor-General to Canada.

So there were three footmen altogether and a steward's room boy, and an odd man. The odd man would do all the odd jobs about the place. The upper servants had their meals in the steward's room and the boy would wait on them and learn to be a footman. There'd be the butler and the housekeeper and the valet and the lady's maid, and the cook *could* go in there, but she very rarely did, because she was so busy in the kitchen. They were allowed to rule the household and rule the roost!

There were six housemaids and a housekeeper, as well as two stillroom maids. They all had their meals in the servants' hall. I always got on very well with the housekeeper. Her uniform was a long black skirt and black blouse and she wore a little white lace cap – and sometimes she would have an apron on (but not very often). She had a belt, and a big bunch of keys to show her position, and she ordered all the provisions for the house. Once a week I had to go to her with a list of all the things that we wanted, and she would get them out. And they said she would be ever so angry if you forgot anything and had to go back another day. You had a special day for doing that. When I first went there people warned me about the housekeeper, and said she was a proper martinet. But I always got on all right with her – she reminded me of my granny. She was quite nice to me, and I never had any trouble at all. The kind of things you would get from the housekeeper were flour and sugar and butter and lard. The lard was in a pigskin, or pig's bladder – they were called 'a bladder of lard'. That was the only place I've ever seen it. You would also get household things – floor cloths, sand and soft soap.

The housekeeper was also the head of the stillroom. Hatfield was the only house where Flo had encountered a stillroom, though its position in the arrangement of grand houses stretched way back into history.

The stillroom maids made cakes for the dining room, and they did all the jams, preserving things, and marmalade, and they did the early morning cups of tea for the gentry. They would also make the toast for breakfast, and bake the bread as well. In the kitchen we just cooked the bacon and eggs, or the kippers or kedgeree, or whatever they had. Working in the stillroom you were more likely to go on to be a housekeeper. I wasn't really conversant with the general practice.

There were four of us in the kitchen. The cook was a person probably in her fifties and there was the head kitchen maid. I was the second one, and then we had a scullery maid. The scullery maid might well have been in her fifties also, but she'd been at Hatfield ever since she left school, because she was brought up in an orphanage. Lady Salisbury had something to do with the orphanage and sometimes took girls from there to work in the house. The scullery maid always stayed at Hatfield; she never moved with us to the other places. Her name was Florence so again I couldn't be called Florence while I was there. They asked me what my second name was, and when I said that was Georgina – well of course that was again too posh for a kitchen maid. I said I was called Ena at one place, but no they didn't like Ena much, so I was called Jean – that was part of Georgina.

At Hatfield – praise be – we had gas! So we had gas rings and there was a big stand in the middle of the kitchen divided into four. The cook would have one part and the head kitchen maid another; the scullery maid would have another and I would have one part. The ovens in the wall had been converted to gas, so we could utilise these. 'Course that was a lot cleaner and there wasn't all the preparation of lighting the stoves like I had gone through before, so that was marvellous. They'd still got their old black-leaded door, and latches to lift up. And of course when we went to London, we had gas there. When we went down to Cranborne in Dorset, we went back to fires, and there was only the head kitchen maid and I went, and we had a scullery maid who came in from the village.

At Hatfield they also had what they called an 'ice cave'. It was specially made so you could freeze such things as soufflés and other special dishes. It had chopped up ice at the bottom and freezing salt to prevent the ice melting. You had to pack it all round, and there was a part in the middle of it where you could put the soufflés. 'Ice soufflés' they called them. Nearly always there was a meat safe and the window would be very fine mesh, so the air could get in.

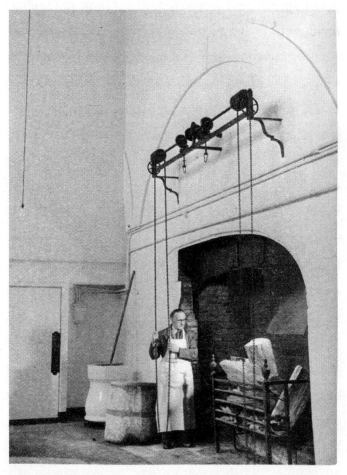

The kitchen contained an old spit, baking ovens in the wall, a meat-chopping block and a brine tub.

There was an old spit hanging in the Hatfield kitchen and there were windows, right up high, so we couldn't see out at all. But in the scullery you could just see out to the front. There were sinks all along here where Florence washed and cleaned the copper pots and pans. They were relined whenever we wanted them to be. I can remember helping Florence sometimes – especially when we had rabbit for the staff. We had ten rabbits to feed all the staff and while she was skinning three, I would do seven. While I was here we had a firm in Wisbech and we used to send all the rabbit skins to them, and I would get so much each skin. That was my perk.

It was quite a big kitchen, and of course it had to be scrubbed every day – and the tables and things, *all* had to be scrubbed. Sometimes, if I wasn't too tired I'd try to do it overnight, so that I hadn't got it to do in the morning. But we were fortunate having the gas here, because we hadn't got the fires to light. Sometimes after lunch you would clean bits of the kitchen floor as well, if anywhere had got particularly dirty. I don't think the cleaning seemed quite so intensive at Hatfield as it was in some of the other places, where they seemed to clean just for the sake of it. At Hatfield – apart from the floors and the tables – you did it when it was necessary. I would get the table all ready then I would scrub the floors, in the morning usually. They were all wooden floors and I did get a terrible splinter of wood down my nail and they had to have the doctor come and take it out for me. That was because the scrubbing brush had worn down rather, and I ought to have had a new one. But as I said, you had to go to the housekeeper for all the stores here, and evidently I didn't ask for one soon enough.

They did provide you with uniform here. We had pink-and-white striped dresses. They were very nice, and little chef's hats – they weren't right tall ones – which you had to have your hair tucked underneath.

My main job again, at Hatfield, was to prepare the staff meals, and you can tell, with all that lot (although we didn't know it at the time) it was quite a big undertaking. There'd be the breakfast for the steward's room and the servants' hall and for us in the kitchen. Mostly, they would have eggs of some kind. Sometimes they would have fish – kippers or something like that, but mostly eggs, with bacon perhaps. And I used to do the vegetables too, for the dining room. The head kitchen maid helped the cook, and of course the scullery maid would prepare the vegetables for the servants, but I would do the cooking of them, and cooked their meals. So I had my day very full.

The staff meals weren't the same as the dining-room meals – 'course they weren't – but they had good meals really, joint of meat for Sundays and cold on the Monday. Perhaps on Tuesday we might have rabbit brought in from the estate, and we'd have rabbit pie or stew. One day a week we'd have fish. Sometimes this was fried and another time perhaps we'd make it into a fish pie.

We had our meals as and when we had time. We did have a little sitting room that was just off our kitchen and we had our meals in there – when we had time to sit down. If you're going to have the servants' lunch at about half past twelve and the dining-room lunch at about quarter past one, you haven't got much time to have your own lunch. You either had it quick beforehand, or else you had it in the middle of the afternoon, when it was past the best. You didn't have a lot of time to use the sitting room but it was lovely just to pop in there and sit down for a few minutes to eat your breakfast – while Mrs Harris, the cook, had perhaps gone up to see her Ladyship, to discuss the menus. The gardeners weren't fed, and they probably lived on the estate.

In addition, however, we had three secretaries who came in every day, and we had to provide lunch for them on trays. Where they ate it I don't know. I never asked! Perhaps they had it in their office or the estate office. I had to do three trays for them, all the steward's room meals and the servants' hall, so I had a busy time.

As a kitchen maid Flo's increasing experience made her more and more useful to the cooks she assisted, particularly as has been suggested, in setting out the cook's working table, and using her knowledge of the menus to keep one step ahead.

In front of the cook there'd be flour. She had a kind of box thing in two halves and it had a lid each side – one side was plain and one was self-raising. She had little canisters with salt and pepper and caster sugar, and the scales were on the table in front of her. I had to see that everything was at hand. All the cook's boards had to be specially scrubbed. You'd put some salt on them and some boiling water. You'd never use soap on the board because if she was chopping up meat or vegetables you couldn't have the taste of soap in the vegetables for her Ladyship could you?

We had a nice case with a glass front and the menu book would be put in there. They were all written in French, so you had to know what the English equivalent was. Now if they had 'Consommé Julienne', I would know that she'd want some vegetables cut into very tiny little strips and cooked, ready to put into the consommé. If it was 'Eggs Florentine' I would know you had to have spinach, and you would cook the spinach and put it through a sieve. They don't have it just chopped up you know. You couldn't have bits of stalk! You had to understand what it was like. I would look at the menus and then I would know what she was doing. If there was a different garnish of some kind I would know what she wanted. At Hatfield I learnt more about menus and I would take notice of what the cook did. My mother said I had an enquiring mind. I was a bit nosey, really. I liked to know what they were doing, as well as me. That's really how I learnt.

The gardener would mostly bring what vegetables he had in the garden. It wasn't so much what we wanted but you used what you had in the season. It wasn't like today, where you have foreign vegetables all the year round. Lord Salisbury, who I worked for, liked very plain food, and he had a milk pudding every day. It didn't matter whatever else was in the dining room, there was a milk pudding made for his Lordship.

At weekends they nearly always had big parties. Ever so many people would come and stay – all the parliamentary people of the time – the Prime Minister and so on. It was nothing to have sixteen or twenty people staying. And they would bring their wives and their wives would bring their lady's maids and the gentlemen would bring their valets and probably a chauffeur. So you would have extra staff in the servants' hall.

At Hatfield there was a wonderful room called the Armoury, with four big tapestries on the wall representing spring, summer, autumn and winter, and there was lots of armour and all that kind of thing. We used to have a man come in, nearly every day, to clean the armour. It was like the Forth Bridge. When he had finished one end of the house, he'd have to go round again!

There were six housemaids, and Rose, the second housemaid, was a particular friend of mine. One day she said, 'The housemaids have got to be up at five tomorrow to scrub the Armoury.'

'Oh,' I said, 'I'll ask the housekeeper if I can come with you.' So I helped scrub the Armoury just so I could see it. I wanted to see the lovely tapestries hanging up. I only scrubbed it once. I had enough scrubbing to do as it was.

* * *

The Armoury had four tapestries showing the seasons. These were woven by the Sheldon Tapestry Weavers in 1611.

There was also a marvellous chapel at Hatfield and we had to go to prayers in the morning, after the servants had had their breakfast and before the dining-room breakfast. The head kitchen maid and I used to take it in turns to go, because one would be left behind looking after the bacon and eggs for the dining room while the others were in chapel, saying their prayers. There'd also be one footman who didn't go. They took it in turns so that one could be on duty at the front door and for the telephone. Occasionally we were all there. Some of the girls didn't like chapel at all. They thought it was an imposition really, but I thought it was lovely. I loved the chapel and that window for one thing, with all the different Bible stories in it. Whenever I think of Hatfield I always think of that window. And I loved seeing the people who I worked for.

Working in the kitchen, as a lowly kitchen maid, you didn't usually see the people of the house and they hardly ever deigned to come down into the kitchen. I shall never forget once, when we were in Arlington Street, Mrs Harris, the cook, had been in to see her Ladyship and we were told that his Lordship was coming into the kitchen, with an architect, because they wanted something done to the place. When Mrs Harris came down from seeing her Ladyship she came into the kitchen and said:

'Our Lord is coming down!' Yes, he did come down, and we stood up meekly.

I only once ever spoke to Lady Salisbury and I never did to his Lordship. But there at Hatfield, his Lordship and her Ladyship came to prayers in the chapel, and you were there with them – a few rows back maybe – so I liked that very much. We'd be all seated in our places before the family came in and we would rise. When the service was over we watched them all walk out then we would walk behind and come out last.

We saw her Ladyship's sister, the Dowager Countess of Airlie. She was a lady-in-waiting to Queen Mary. She was a dignified and stately lady, very much in the style of Queen Mary. She looked and dressed like Queen Mary. She often used to come and visit when she wasn't on duty at Buckingham Palace. Anthony Eden used to come to Hatfield and all the top people in the cabinet, and they would come to chapel too. That's how

I saw all these people that you read about in the newspapers.

I wasn't so keen coming on Wednesdays or Fridays because we always had the Litany that day – that was a bit beyond me – but otherwise I loved it. It really started me off. The clergyman or the curate would come from Hatfield and take the prayers, and we'd have hymns. When we went to London we didn't have services in the house there, but we did in Cranborne. We went in the dining room there and his Lordship would say the prayers. I laughed and said we should have had prayers in London, because that's where you want them more, don't you? You could be more led astray in London than you could in Cranborne or Hatfield!

In the general run of things, the kitchen staff would tend not to mix with the other staff, but Flo was probably an exception to the rule:

It happened to me. I mixed with them because, if there was a dance or anything in the village, several of the servants would go, and the younger girl who worked in the stillroom, she would go and some of the younger housemaids. We would all go to the dances. I was very friendly with the second footman and he used to take me. We used to play golf as well because there was a lovely golf course at Hatfield. Where he got the clubs from I didn't enquire into – you don't go into that.

One day, when I went to the housekeeper with the list of what we needed that day, she asked me if I would like to go to the Servants' Ball. 'Oh yes, I'd love it!' 'Who would I like to go with me?' Well the second housemaid, Rose, she was a very nice girl and we had Stanley my favourite footman, and the under chauffeur to take us. But oh, the head kitchen maid was furious because she wasn't asked to go – but she never went to dances normally. I thought it was only fair. I was thrilled to bits. The ball was at a neighbouring house and this neighbour was some relative I think to Lord Salisbury. They were inviting four servants from Hatfield House.

Before then though I cycled from Hatfield to

London – the traffic on the A1 wasn't quite like it is today – to Selfridges. I put my bike by the railings in Portman Square, at the back of Selfridges, and went in. I bought myself some material to make a long dress because they were all the rage then. I got some pale lilac material and made a dress with a V-neck. It had two little frills to make the short sleeves and then a long skirt from the waist, and two frills at the bottom and a bunch of violets there. I made that to go to the Servants' Ball, which was fantastic. We had a wonderful time.

You had to have a special pass to go out, because they had night watchmen round the grounds, and there were Alsatian dogs, so you had to let them know the date you'd got a pass for. We'd be late home going to the dance.

I remember too we had a big Fireman's Ball. They had their own brigade, and their own fire engine at Hatfield. People on the estate all manned it. I remember we all went to this Fireman's Ball and it was from about eight in the evening until about five in the morning. I know the footmen came home, had a bath and changed into their uniforms straight away and went on duty. I think we did have a few minutes' rest before we started to get up at half past six. Some of the things we used to do like going to dances – the young people don't seem as if they've got the energy like we had! We worked hard all day long, sometimes until gone nine o'clock at night, or ten, then we'd go up and change and cycle off to the dance.

The year 1935 was King George V and Queen Mary's Silver Jubilee and there were lots of big activities going on in London that year. I think they had a service at St Paul's, which Lord and Lady Salisbury attended, and there was a big procession, all through the streets. We could go from Arlington Street to St James's, which was the next street, and watch all the processions. There was a marvellous concert in the Albert Hall – a Royal Command Concert – but not the stars of the theatre or anything like that. I think there were two men and two ladies from each county from different choirs to make up a big choir. They had all the traditional songs. Mrs Harris, the cook, had a brother who was picked from Dorset, and he had tickets, so I went with Mrs Harris to the Royal Command Performance in the Albert Hall. Mrs Harris also had a cousin who was a chauffeur to Princess Beatrice, who lived in Kensington Palace, and I remember us going round one day to where he lived.

The next year King George V died, so we saw the funeral. His Lordship went to the funeral and they went from London to Windsor Castle. I know that was a very sad day after the lovely year we had for the Silver Jubilee.

I also remember going to a concert at the Queen's Hall in London, and I will never forget the girl who played the violin. I don't know who she was. She had a gold lamé dress and she was playing this instrument and I can picture now the spotlight shining on her dress. All round the room were mirrors and you could see her reflection.

I was at Hatfield just over a year. I came in the January 1935 and I left in the February 1936. I left really because my mother was ill. I'd had a little half-brother, and this child had died. So I went home to look after Mother. I was in London when I gave my notice in – 'cause you had to give a month's notice. Lady Salisbury asked for me to be taken up to the drawing room to see her when I was going to leave Hatfield. She said that Mrs Harris had been very pleased with all the work that I'd done, and would be only too pleased to have me back. So they couldn't have given me a bad reference.

I didn't really think about going back to Hatfield however. After Mother got better, I thought I would try and get a job in Norfolk somewhere, so I could get home more easily – perhaps once a week – to see how she was getting on. I'd been home about a month and Mother was a lot better so I put my name down at a local agency to get another job. What I *would* have liked was to get a job up in Scotland, where they had the grouse parties and all that kind of thing. I wished I could have gone to a big house, or a castle, as a kitchen maid even.

I know we are all supposed to be equal, but these establishments did give you an insight into a different way of life. Somebody asked me once if living in a big house like that, and seeing all the marvellous furniture and silver and everything they had, was I ever envious? I never was really. I was always very interested, but I can't ever remember wanting it.

The 'Health and Beauty' movement found a keen recruit in Flo. 'One day when his Lordship wasn't here and the gardeners weren't about, we went out in the garden and I stood on one of the statues – posed there in my outfit.'

CHAPTER FIVE

Blickling Hall

Philip Kerr, 11th Marquess of Lothian, the owner of Blickling, was at the very centre of world affairs, and greatly respected. Lord Lothian was a Liberal, and as Lloyd George's secretary, was of immense value to the Prime Minister at the Paris Peace Conference and in the drafting of the Treaty of Versailles. It was said that President Wilson 'treated him, not as a prime minister's secretary, but as if he were an emissary to the Conference, and a very important one.' With no previous diplomatic background, he was appointed to the key position of Washington Ambassador. Churchill described him as 'our greatest ambassador to the United States'.

When I was at home one day a lady came to the door and asked if I was Miss Copeland, and I said 'yes'. She asked if she could come in and she told me she was Miss O'Sullivan and she was secretary/housekeeper to the Marquess of Lothian, at Blickling Hall. The cook there had walked out in a bad temper, and they'd got two weekend parties that his Lordship had arranged and they hadn't got a cook to cook the meals. Would I come and do it for these two weekends? I said I couldn't possibly do that, as I'd only been a kitchen maid. 'But,' she said, 'you've worked at Hatfield House and you'd know what to do.' Anyway, his Lordship only wanted plain and simple things. I didn't say that at the time but I had mainly cooked for the servants and not for the dining room. She felt sure that I would be all right, and my mother persuaded me to go. Mother said, 'You're not going under false pretences. If the lady is desperate, why don't you go and help her!' So of course, off I went – for a fortnight.

At the end of the two weekends (which passed off very well), Miss O'Sullivan told me that his Lordship was very pleased with what I had cooked and would I consider stopping on. I didn't really want to do that because I didn't think I was experienced enough.

She said that what I had cooked for his Lordship was very nice, but I explained that there were lots of things that I hadn't done. I wanted to improve myself and have someone to teach me other things. She asked me what kinds of things I wanted to learn, and I said that I'd made buns or big slab cake for the staff but I'd never made cakes, or iced cakes, for the drawing-room teas – anything fancy. Oh, that was no problem at all – she would send me to the 'Tech', in Norwich, and I could go there one day a week and learn what I wanted to learn.

It was really against what I wanted to do. I didn't want to stay there, but I stayed anyway and I used to go to the Tech. I learnt all different sorts of cake-making and icing cakes, as well as different kinds of puddings – a bit more elaborate than the ones I had been used to. I was there about a term or so. It was the only time I had a teacher to myself. I asked her what recipe book I should have, and she told me, *The Fine Art of Cookery*, and that's what I bought.

His Lordship paid for the lessons and they paid my bus fare to Norwich. I used to cycle from Blickling to Aylsham and could catch the bus there. I have to admit that sometimes I used to bike all the way and save my bus fare!

Blickling Hall was built 1616–27 for Sir Henry Hobart.
Anne Boleyn is said to have lived in an earlier house on this site.

Flo found herself in charge of the kitchen at Blickling somewhat against her better judgement. Very unusually, she was still in her early twenties and most cooks, certainly in large houses, would be in their forties or fifties. It was a different situation perhaps for the rest of the staff to have to deal with as well. The accepted rules of the hierarchy, and of promotion, had been broken. It was interesting that when researchers from the National Trust were looking for former servants to interview, they managed to find a few butlers and some housemaids, but Flo was the only cook. Flo quite understood why, because her age was half that of the average cook in that kind of position.

Getting the job at Blickling I just feel was an accident. I was the only person they had at the agency who had any experience of a large house, so they suggested me. They evidently had good references. I don't think I could say there was resentment at Blickling. The head housemaid wasn't at all supportive because she was older than me. What she might have resented was my age, not that I couldn't do the work. I was much younger than she was. I was never given the courtesy title of 'Mrs' there, like most cooks were. I was always 'Flo', but I didn't mind that at all. I wouldn't have had quite the respect an elder person would have had but I don't think they made things awkward. I think the butler was quite pleasant. He was called Mr Dunning and we called him that. We didn't call him 'sir'. Mr Dunning lived in a cottage not far from the park gates. He had a wife and a family, so if he had any time off, he'd go home.

There was a footman, who used to come from Aylsham, and he lived in the house. As far as I can remember, he had a little room near the pantry. There was an odd man called Sidney Perts. We called him an odd man but he was a nice gentleman really. He was an older person and his family had lived in Blickling for years and years. They lived in a cottage near the big barn. The odd man would bring all the wood baskets and the coal scuttles in, for the different fireplaces. He would wait on the staff in the servants' hall while the butler and the footman would take in the dining-room meals. Sometimes the odd man would help in the dining room as well. I remember he always came into the kitchen with a tray to take the servants' meals to the servants' hall, but it was all kinds of odd jobs that he did. Apart from the kitchen maid and the scullery maid (my friend Kath) the other servants weren't allowed in the kitchen, unless they had business to come in for – no more than I was allowed in their part. The housemaids had their own sitting room, the kitchen servants had their own sitting room and the men servants were mostly kept in the pantry. We didn't mix very much.

There were three housemaids: the head housemaid was Irene, and the other two were Doris and Violet. I think they were two sisters. When they left we had another two sisters come. They did all the housework. They would polish all the fireplaces up, lay the fires in the different rooms, make the beds and sweep and dust. I don't believe they had any hoovers. The housemaids did my room but the kitchen maid and the scullery maid (they shared a room) they had to do their own. There were three of us in the kitchen so that was nine servants altogether, which was ever so much smaller than Hatfield. There were six housemaids there alone, and they needed them too.

Here the kitchen was so lovely because you could look out onto the gardens. In most of the houses where I've been you were all closed in and you couldn't see out of the windows at all, so you didn't see a garden like this. We were very fortunate especially in the springtime when the magnolia was out. It was beautiful, with the white flowers tinged with pink, and blue grape hyacinths underneath – a perfect picture. I wished I could paint. (I have done since, but I'm not very good. I'll have to stick to cooking!)

We didn't have an Aga and we didn't have gas either. We still had a big kitchen range, but of course it never bothered me because I didn't have to light it. Kath had to do that; she was a good girl with the fire. In the range we had two ovens, one on each side. All the cooking for the house was done on the range, but the water heater was separate. The kitchen maids used to get up quite early and light the range. You would have to clean the flues out and all that so many times a week. The range had to be black-leaded and the shiny parts would be all 'emery-papered'. The kitchen maid would do that every morning. They started work at half past six – not just got up then! I got up at seven o'clock. Sometimes if his Lordship was here with a big party, I might be up a bit earlier, because I always used to make the bread rolls for breakfast. There'd be eggs of some kind with bacon, and there'd be fish – perhaps haddock, kippers or kedgeree. There might be kidneys or sausages, and cold ham on the sideboard. In the old copper utensils I used to make marmalade that lasted the whole year – a certain quantity at a time – about a dozen oranges that would be. Packets of sugar used to come from the Army and Navy Stores, in London. We had preserving sugar, lump sugar, granulated and caster.

We used to have large kettles that we had to fill up at night for the housemaids to fill the hot water bottles, for the beds. And we used to be so angry because they would fill the bottles up and leave the kettles empty!

We had a plain wooden table which was scrubbed every day – twice a day sometimes. The kitchen maid would scrub the kitchen table, and the kitchen floor. But the scullery maid would do the higher part of the kitchen – that was her domain! She would scrub the passages, and the larder. She would do all the 'donkey work'. She would do all the vegetables and the washing-up and the kitchen maid would do the vegetables for the dining room as well as the cooking for the servants' hall.

I always tried to treat the other kitchen staff

kindly, as I'd mostly been treated. I wouldn't be sarcastic or be horrid to them, and I tried to show them things. You didn't have many gadgets, not in them days. You had to whisk by hand. You didn't even have wheel whisks. That's why we wanted girls to help – to prepare the vegetables and do the washing-up.

One thing we had at Blickling was a *fridge*! That was the first place I'd ever had a fridge. And that I think was mainly because his Lordship was a teetotaller, and he loved orange juice to drink, and of course that all had to be fresh oranges. We had crates of oranges delivered locally and the kitchen maid used to squeeze them and put the juice in a lovely glass jug. She'd do it overnight and put it in the fridge ready for breakfast. Then after breakfast she'd do another jug all ready for lunch, and after lunch another jug ready for dinner at night. I think the purpose of the fridge was just to make the orange juice nice and cool. I'd had an icebox before, a big lead-lined chest, but at Blickling it was a fridge for the first time – one of the old-fashioned sort, ever so tall.

Miss O'Sullivan, the housekeeper, she liaised between me and his Lordship. I mainly decided what the menus would be. I used to write out what I thought would be a good idea and Miss O'Sullivan used to come down in the morning and we'd talk these things over. All the menus were written in French. I'd learnt all this, being a kitchen maid. I would plan the whole menu for the weekend, for example, and see if she thought that was all right. Mostly she agreed with what I had written down. We used to have soup first, then fish and then meat and sweet, and sometimes savoury as well. If his Lordship had only one or two guests for lunch they might only have two courses. If there was a big party then they had a starter first – hors d'oeuvres or something.

If you was preparing consommé, that would have been a couple of days' job, 'cause you would have your bones first from the butcher and you'd boil them up and strain them overnight. We always had a big stockpot boiling with the bones and things, and you strained that up so that the fat would all settle on the top. You'd take all the fat off the next day. Then you'd have your stock and you'd have your shin of beef all cut up, and onions and carrots and celery, things like that, all put in, to make the consommé. After that had cooked for an hour or so that would all be strained off. Then it would be cleared with egg white as well, so it was shiny. In some places I would have put some sherry in the consommé, but I didn't at Blickling because his Lordship was a teetotal gentleman. We didn't use alcohol in the cooking – but his Lordship had it for his friends.

The head gardener would come and say what fruit and vegetables he'd got in the garden and what he could send in for me to use. One of the under gardeners would bring it all in for me. The kitchen garden was in the walled area just the other side of the Lime Tree Walk – but of course I never did go in the kitchen garden. There was a head gardener, Mr Willey, and he and his wife and little girl lived in one of the buildings near the front of the hall towards the yew hedges. Near where he lived was where the old kitchen used to be but of course we never worked in it. There used to be an underground tunnel to come through for the dining room, but we were in the part where the kitchen is now, although it wasn't exactly the same.

One evening we would have consommé followed by fish of some kind. If you had consommé, which is brown, you'd probably have a white fish. You might have a crown of lamb or chicken done with grapes. Mostly the chicken was carved up. One of his Lordship's favourite dishes was an American recipe called Chicken Maryland – where they have the corn pancakes and banana. We'd often have a soufflé – mostly cold sweets at night – or ice cream. And fruit of course. His Lordship was very fond of fruit. Sometimes they would have savouries – cheese, or 'angels on horseback' [oysters wrapped with bacon on a little crouton].

I would order all the things that I wanted from the trades-people, who came from Aylsham. There was Ward & George's the grocers, in the market place. The grocer would come down and take the order. Mr Partridge, the butcher, would also come here to the kitchen and take the order. Mr Balls was the fishmonger. You could ring them up or get the secretary to ring them up. Somebody would be down with a little van, if we needed quite a lot, if it was going to be a big party, or a boy on a bike with a big basket to deliver it. There was never any hesitation about that, and like the greengrocers, Ewings, who we had the oranges from – if you wanted an extra crate of oranges, and he hadn't got them in the shop, he'd get them somewhere, and bring them. Milk and cream, and some butter, came from Brick Kiln Farm, a Mrs Matthewson – her husband used to farm there. They were lovely people. We loved visiting them if we ran short of milk any time. We would go, just for the pleasure of going and talking to them.

Flo remembers her accommodation well. She had a bedroom with a view.

There are two turrets at the ends, and my bedroom was the next room to the left-hand turret as you face the house. I had a doorway and I could walk from my bedroom into the turret. There was a lovely view but the window was quite high up – you had to get right near the window. There was a kind of a little balcony outside it, but I never did go out of the window. I had a bed, a little table at the side and a chair, but my wardrobe was through in the turret itself. There was only just my wardrobe in the tower.

There was a sitting room when we had an hour or two off. We had a wireless in here and I had my sewing machine. I used to do some sewing sometimes, or have my knitting. You could look out onto the park. We really had a lovely outlook.

I remember going up to the library once when I worked here 'cause they were going to take all the books out and dust them all. And I *volunteered* to help, because I wanted to go and have a look. I wanted to see what the library was like.

Flo never saw or heard the ghost, but others apparently did!

I'm too 'matter of fact' a person. I wouldn't see a ghost if there *was* one. But somebody saw a ghost. One weekend we had two waiters who came from London and they slept in a bedroom right at the furthest end near another turret, and they went home next day because they were too frightened to sleep in there another night. We all went up there to see if we could see anything or hear anything, but we never did.

Lady Nancy Astor, a friend of Lord Lothian, perhaps thought on one occasion that there were ghostly footsteps treading the floor above her ceiling:

The scullery maid used to bring me a cup of tea every morning before I got up. I'd really got to the top of the ladder then! Lady Astor once said to the butler, 'Is the cook a very big person?' And he said 'No, not really.' And she said, 'Well I hear her footsteps going round the room every morning.' My room was on the floor above hers and that was the scullery maid bringing me my cup of tea.

Lord Lothian did not live at Blickling all the time. He had an apartment in London. Two of his greatest friends were Lord and Lady Astor. She used to bring her lady's maid, and he brought his chauffeur and valet. The thing I always remember about the valet was when he used to make his Lordship a pot of tea first thing in the morning, he would always warm the cups. I used to think to myself, by the time you get to the bedroom they will be cold again. Lady Astor came quite regularly. Lord Lothian had quite a lot of American friends who used to come, and Lady Astor was one. She was the first lady in Parliament.

I think I only saw Lord Lothian about twice, and I was there over three years. There wasn't a lot of contact. I think he was a nice sort of gentleman but they weren't brought up to be friendly with the staff, were they? The butler, for example, might have got through to him. He would have had more to talk to him about.

I remember the butler came down once and said to me, 'His Lordship was talking about you at lunch.' 'Good gracious!' He'd had the rector to lunch. As a girl I'd always been brought up a Methodist. At Woodhall, Hilgay, we were allowed to go to church on a Sunday evening. At Hatfield, as I've said, we would go to the chapel there, and the rector would come in for the prayers. I got used to the liturgy of the church and I rather liked it. You knew where you were. When I went to Blickling I thought I would like to be confirmed. So I asked the rector and I went to confirmation classes. I think the kitchen maid came with me as well. The rector was thrilled to bits. He was telling his Lordship all about it – and 'what an intelligent young lady I was'!

I would have liked to have heard them talking sometimes – what they had to say. It would have been nice to be a fly on the wall.

I thoroughly enjoyed Blickling, once I got into it. Working there you never quite knew how many people to expect. His Lordship was in London most of the week, but weekends he came down here. In most establishments you would get into a routine so that you more or less knew what you were going to do each day. It was never like that with his Lordship. You never quite knew what was going to happen. Sometimes his Lordship might come down on his own, but that was very rare indeed. Another time he might bring two or three friends, or somebody from Parliament that he wanted to discuss world affairs with. I know Parliamentary people did like coming because things were building up on the Continent weren't they, towards a war.

1936 – that was the year of the abdication crisis. The old King had died and King Edward wanted to marry Wallis Simpson. Stanley Baldwin was the Prime Minister at the time, and of course he couldn't go out of the country, so the Marquess, being a very hospitable gentleman, invited him to stay at Blickling Hall for his holiday. So the Prime Minister came with his secretaries and chauffeur and detectives. And Mrs Baldwin came as well. I think they were only there about three weeks.

Before they went home, the butler had to take me through to the drawing room because Mrs Baldwin wanted to thank me for the nice meals. She was very appreciative and I remember she gave me a pound – and another pound to share between the kitchen maid and the scullery maid. Farmworkers only got about twenty-five shillings a week so a pound was quite a lot of money. My husband always used to say 'you ought to have framed that!' When I first came to Blickling I think I had about fifty pounds a year, the next year that was raised up to fifty-five pounds and the next year to sixty pounds. Having all my keep, I was quite well off really.

One weekend there was a party of Americans who were going to sail on the *Queen Mary*, and hadn't for some reason or other. I can't remember if they had a strike on the ship or if there was something the matter with the engines, but the ship was delayed and they couldn't sail just when they expected. So 'course his Lordship invited them to come to stay at Blickling for the weekend. I thought that was most extraordinary – to come all the way from Southampton to Blickling. But two or three hundred miles is nothing to Americans. So along they came, and we had to provide for them – all in a hurry. But you could always ring up for extra provisions. I think on that occasion Miss O'Sullivan had to ring up the butcher, the baker and the candlestick maker! But we managed it and it all went off quite all right. I can't remember many catastrophes we had, not in the cooking line.

It was a good job I had gone to the classes in Norwich because one day, just after lunch, the butler came down – you can tell how removed the family are from real work – and he said, could they have a birthday cake for tea, 'cause it was somebody's birthday!' Just like that – wave a wand. Fortunately the kitchen maid said she'd made a fruit cake for the staff that day, so I commandeered that and used it. How I'd got the icing sugar in the place, I can't think. Anyway, I know I iced it and I sent it in. It was a good job I'd learnt a bit about doing these kinds of things. You never knew what to expect with his Lordship. After that I used to keep a cake ready, just in case!

I remember once we had a big party. It was some folk-dance celebration and they had big marquees on the grass. They had come to do this folk dancing – you know: one-two-three – four-five-six – seven-eight-nine – turn the circle. It was lovely to watch. His Lordship thought it would be nice if we provided the tea, so we did tea for about five hundred people, from all over the county. The housemaid never did get over that. She said, 'Some cooks would have nearly torn their hair out – but it never made any difference to you. You just got on with it and made the cakes.' The kitchen maid made cakes, and I made cakes of all kinds. I thought to myself, 'I made a ginger cake when I went to the Tech, I'll make a ginger sponge now.' Of course it was made with plain flour and bicarbonate of soda. The recipe said one spoonful, but being a very generous soul I put in a bit extra. That will raise up better! But you have to be very careful with bicarb, you see. It looked lovely in the oven and of course it 'ris' up ever so well, but when I got it out of the oven it sunk all in the middle. Oh dear, I thought. Well I'd better make another one and see how it goes. So I added a bit of extra bicarbonate and the same thing happened again. I thought I can't waste it. I'm a bit like my mum – she was a very economical person. The outside of the cake was all right. It was the middle that was stodgy. So I cut the outside into little squares and put them on a plate and sent that in. I got rid of the middle in the pig bucket.

The next day was one of the rare occasions I saw his Lordship. He came down to the kitchen and thanked me very much indeed for the wonderful tea that I'd provided. He particularly liked the gingerbread and would I send some up to the drawing room for his tea! We had enough food for the five hundred and I think nearly everybody in the village had a little bag of cakes afterwards. We had masses of cakes. My catering wasn't that good. I had enough for everyone – but I'd overdone it.

To an outsider the preparation of food for large numbers, even 'sixteen for lunch' would throw most people into a panic – particularly in judging how much food to use. Was there any 'table of quantities'? How was it done?

With meat, for the ladies it would be about two ounces and four to six ounces for the men. If they were having fish before the meat and they were having both courses, they wouldn't want such a big helping. Experience helped you, I think. I had never seen a cookery book until I went to Blickling and I'd never seen the cooks use one. They'd always been taught, I suppose, how to make these things, and they knew it all in their head. But you see, not doing cooking for the dining room, or teas for the drawing room, I found it harder.

You could always use things up. If you had too

much meat sent in, you could always make a curry, or something like that, for the servants' supper, or make a cottage pie with it.

The Women's Institute was always a great attraction to Flo, and here she is seen (seated far right) at the start of an Aylsham WI outing.

As always Flo took advantage of any opportunity to socialise. The WI also provided interesting activities to promote fitness.

One meeting we had a lady come from 'The League of Health and Beauty', and she gave demonstrations of all the exercises. So we thought we'd have classes – and of course I *had* to go to that! I made my satin blouse, and little shorts and we used to do our exercises. The kitchen maid and the scullery maid came as well. We had a whale of a time. I think we laughed more to see ourselves doing this than we did the exercises. And one day when his Lordship wasn't here and the gardeners weren't about, we went out in the garden and I stood on one of the statues – posed there, in my outfit! I always used to say – 'I've got the health, I am going for the beauty.' My son asked me why I left off going!

Apart from 'Health and Beauty' costumes they wore the usual uniform and at Blickling they had to provide this themselves:

The kitchen maid and the scullery maid would have blue print dresses with white aprons and white caps. I had a white dress with a white apron and a white cap and black shoes and stockings. The only place where I had my uniform provided was at Hatfield. Otherwise I always had to have my own uniform.

* * *

In 1939 his Lordship went to America as Ambassador. We were all going to leave, but I was still there. I was in the kitchen at Blickling. I can remember it quite clearly – I'll never forget it. Mr Chamberlain saying we are at war with Germany, listening to the wireless and hearing him talk about that – very sad. I can't remember exactly when we left, but I suppose it was before that Christmas. Then his Lordship let the RAF have the Hall, for their officers. Miss O'Sullivan still stayed there in her flat, but they didn't keep any staff on at all. And of course Lord Lothian died in 1940, so he never came back to it.

Even if the war hadn't happened we had to leave because his Lordship went to America. The head housemaid was approached to go to America. She said to me one day, if she went to America would I consider going? She knew they had a chef at the Embassy but would I go, as a kitchen maid? I didn't really want to leave my mother – I thought the world of my mother. And I was friends with a nice auburn-haired young man – my future husband. So I didn't go, and she didn't go either. I've always said – 'cause his Lordship died of food poisoning – he should have took me, then he wouldn't have got it!

Pageant poster. 'Aylsham church wanted a lot of money for a new roof and they had this big pageant, at Blickling. "The Masque of Ann Boleyn" it was called – a marvellous pageant, and Queen Mary came to it.'

CHAPTER SIX

Cooking Up a Royal Treat

It goes without saying that the highlight of the three years Flo spent as cook at Blickling Hall was the visit of Queen Mary, the widow of George V. Cooking for royalty was a new experience for Flo.

I took it in my stride, I think. Aylsham Church wanted a lot of money for a new roof, or part of their roof, and they had this big pageant, at Blickling. 'The Masque of Anne Boleyn', it was called – a marvellous pageant, and Queen Mary came to it. It was all about Anne Boleyn, because the Boleyn family are supposed to have lived at Blickling. They couldn't have lived in this hall because it wasn't built until a long while after she died. Of course we had Queen Mary for lunch and tea, and with the Queen you know what an entourage they have. We knew she was coming some while beforehand, and Miss O'Sullivan had been in touch with Clarence House. You had to send a couple of menus to see what the Queen would like, and what she would eat. You couldn't serve up something she didn't like, or give her something that didn't agree with her. I had to suggest the ideas for the two menus. It was either chicken or lamb, and it was chicken they asked for.

There was the Lord Lieutenant of the county, the High Sheriff and the Bishop of Norwich. You name it – all the bigwigs came, and one or two of the people who actually took part in the pageant. That's the only time that I ever cooked for royalty. But once was enough, really!

To see the wonderful table settings, Flo and the staff were allowed a peep before the Queen arrived.

That was the only time I ever went in the dining room. The gardeners always used to do the flowers in the Hall in them days, and they had made beautiful arrangements, in red, white and blue, like posies. There was all the silver and the glass, and the table was polished up to the nines. It was really beautiful. And we were privileged to go and have a look at it – the table where Queen Mary was going to sit.

In 2004 Flo, then aged ninety-one, was asked to make a radio programme for BBC Radio 4, about her life in service, especially at Hatfield and Blickling. She returned to these houses, over sixty years since having worked in them. At Blickling she was delighted to be asked to replicate the main course she had cooked for the memorable 'Royal' lunch in the summer of 1938.

We had a kind of baked, stuffed egg for the first course and then we had the chicken dish – 'Poulet Chaud et Froid' (chicken hot and cold). I could write it down a lot better than I can say it! It was cold chicken done in a white sauce with aspic, and different salads. I think there was spaghetti in the middle of the chicken pieces on the dish – spaghetti with such things as peppers and sweetcorn. As I have said, you would usually prepare some of the food overnight and some the next day. In the morning you would prepare a lot of things for the night-time meals. I would have cooked the pieces of chicken the night before, and I would have made all the dish the night before, the sauce as well. If not, you wouldn't have had a lot of time to get it really cold. I would have got the butcher to take the breasts from the *'petits poussins'* (little chickens). I wouldn't have to do that. The butcher would take the breasts off – but I would ask him to bring the bones as well. You'd use your bones for making stock.

You'd put your chicken in a flat dish with stock and onion, and some herbs. You'd let that cook very gently in the oven – like poached chicken. You'd just let it get cooked. You wouldn't want it to fall to pieces – just cooked enough to eat. You'd take all those breasts of chicken out of the stock and put them on another tray and put it in the fridge to get really cold overnight.

There were peaches for the pudding that had been grown in the garden – white ones I think they were. They were just cooked, halved and served on little pieces of sponge cake with a little raspberry sauce over them. And there was a mousse went in as well, with the peaches.

Now I'm just melting the margarine – of course

you can use butter if you like. In 1938 I would have used butter. You used butter for nearly everything in those days. You didn't use margarine very much at all. I'm adding the flour to make a roux – the basis of the sauce. You have to keep stirring it. I didn't want no lumps in it – not for Queen Mary! It's thickening up. That was quite hot on the range. Talk about slaving over a hot stove – that weren't the word. You used a 'bain-marie' a lot. [A bain-marie was once an indispensable part of large kitchens and consisted of half a dozen or more lidded pots in various sizes which stood in a shallow, wide tin of warm water. It was especially suited to making sauces and was a gentler form of heat from the range.] You'd make your sauce early and you'd have a pan filled with hot water. You stood it on the side of the stove and put your saucepans in, to keep them hot.

That's coming quite thick now. I thought because I left off stirring that I was going to have a lump in it! I've got a whisk anyway. I'll add a bit more milk. There was a tamis cloth to get rid of lumps. The only place I used a tamis cloth was at Hatfield. It was a very fine cloth and it would need two of us, the head kitchen maid and I. We'd put the soup, for example, into the cloth, over a bowl and we'd work it through the cloth with a couple of wooden spoons – so it came out very fine indeed. There was also a 'hair sieve' and most people thought that was quite enough – but at Hatfield you had to have a tamis cloth.

You put the sauce over the chicken, then you would let that get cold in the fridge. You might decorate it with little diamond shapes cut from cucumber skin. With a brush you would baste it all over with aspic, which had been melted in a saucepan, to give it a shiny finish. It should be quite smooth on the top – it shouldn't have no lines. Then back in the fridge.

We used to decorate it too with pimentos or truffles. We had cutters in shapes like hearts and diamonds, clubs and spades, so you could do hearts and diamonds with pimentos and clubs and spades with truffles.

For the sixteen guests for this special lunch you would have had two servings of everything.

You generally did it for eight. If there happened to be just ten you wouldn't do two dishes, but mainly you would do things for eight. If there were twelve people for lunch you would do two sixes. You'd have eight pieces of chicken on one dish and eight on another, and you'd have the butler and the head footman to serve it – or perhaps waiters came in. They would serve the lady of the house first and then the principal guest. They used to help themselves to the meat – presented to them on their left-hand side. Serving things up in the dining room was different from what they do in restaurants and what they do on the television nowadays. It was differently presented. You didn't put one piece on a plate and garnish that – you garnished the dish.

As his Lordship wasn't married, his sister would sometimes come and stay. She was Lady Cecil Kerr, and another sister sometimes came. They would be served first. In the case of Queen Mary, she would be the first. The footman would come round with the salads and they helped themselves to whatever salads or vegetables they wanted.

And after lunch when the Queen was going out to see the pageant, Flo and the others did get to see the royal visitor – through the window. If the photographs in the local press are evidence, the pageant was quite spectacular.

Lady Hastings was Lady Boleyn and Lady Hastings' daughter was Anne Boleyn. Lord Walpole was Lord Percy. Anne Boleyn and this Lord Percy were very much in love before they ever thought of her marrying the King. Henry VIII took part, and there was also Cardinal Wolsey. In this pageant King Henry came down to ask the Boleyn family for the hand of Anne in marriage (I don't think he *asked*). There were all the gentry from round and about.

The actors who were supposed to be the village people put on a play to entertain the King, like they used to have the Mummers Play years ago. And it was all done in lovely broad Norfolk. Mr Broad, who lived in Heydon, was St George. When I came to Heydon to live, and I worked at The Grange, Mr Broad used to come there, and I often laughed at him and said, 'Here comes the Turkish Knight. I've come from Turkish lands to fight. Here comes St George from Hampton Court, he's only got a wooden sword!' Mr Broad always used to answer me back by saying: 'A wooden sword, you dirty dog!' When they were rehearsing I could say it nearly all off. I always remember the Turkish Knight.

This is how the local newspaper reported Queen Mary's visit, and the Blickling masque:

QUEEN MARY AT THE MASQUE

Queen Mary was warmly cheered by the 300 performers in the 'Masque of Anne Boleyn' when she attended the last of the afternoon performances at Blickling Hall yesterday. The audience of over 1200 people joined enthusiastically in the applause as her Majesty, who was all in white, with a white plumed toque, walked from the Hall to her seat in the Royal box in one of the stands.

After the National Anthem had been played there was a charming incident. Roland Price, the little boy who played the part of Cupid so boldly in the prologue and epilogue, stepped up to the Royal box and presented her Majesty with a bouquet of red and white carnations.

Queen Mary's presence set the seal on the success of the masque, to which she had already given her patronage. The performances, which ended last night, were in aid of the Aylsham Church Restoration Fund.

It is understood that her Majesty was entertained to luncheon by Lord Lothian at Blickling Hall, before attending the performance. A few moments before three o'clock, her Majesty came out of the main entrance of the Hall chatting to Lord Lothian. Among others in the party which followed her to the stand were Lord Hastings, the Home Secretary (Sir Samuel Hoare), H.M. Lieutenant for Norfolk (Mr Colman), and the Bishop of Norwich. Lord Hastings sat at Queen Mary's right hand throughout the performance. Both Lady Hastings, and her daughter, the Hon. Jean Astley, had prominent parts in the masque, Miss Astley as Anne Boleyn and Lady Hastings as her mother, Lady Boleyn.

Two scenes from 'The Masque of Anne Boleyn', performed in
the summer of 1938 in front of Blicking Hall.
The lower picture shows the mummers' play with
St George and the Dragon.

The next day, or the day after, his Lordship came down again to the kitchen, and thanked me very much for all that they'd had. That was the second time I saw him.

And when, for her Radio 4 programme, 'Poulet Chaud et Froid' was once again ready to serve, it looked every bit as good as it must have done back in 1938. The programme presenter, Adrian Bell, and the cook had of course to sample the food. Adrian Bell was very enthusiastic and declared: 'Mrs Wadlow, you have not lost your touch!'

Mr and Mrs Bob Wadlow, covered in confetti after their marriage in St Peter Mancroft Church, Norwich.

CHAPTER SEVEN

Wartime and Later Life

Flo Wadlow had coped amazingly well with the demands of the important job of cook at Blickling in her early twenties, and doubtless had it not been for the war, she might well have stayed. In her last two posts she had realised her ambition to work for the aristocracy, and had even had a brief taste of cooking for royalty, although working for the Royal Family had never been a particular aim!

I don't think I ever thought as high as that. They said that the people in control, the heads of the households, weren't very easy people to work for. You always found, in service, or nearly always, it wasn't the lady and gentleman who caused any trouble that there was. It was the cook or the butler who were the 'top dogs'. They were going to be bowed down to. You had to treat them with respect. I never minded that, it was all part and parcel of it. I was good at my job and they were good at theirs and that's all that mattered. You're a cog in the wheel really, to help things along. At Hatfield we were ever so busy and we worked ever so hard – hardly ever had a Sunday off – but it was nearly all worthwhile, when I think back.

I was always taught – my mother told me – to be deferential to older people, and people in high positions, like you would be to your schoolteacher or the parson, and the Lady of the Manor. Of course you would be. It came naturally to me, but I don't think it came naturally to all the staff. My mother said it didn't cost anything to be polite; she was always strict about that. I wasn't the type of girl who would answer them back, and if they asked me to do anything I tried to do it to please them. Well there was a better atmosphere if they were pleased, wasn't there? So I did work hard on public relations because I think it makes life so much nicer, and things work so much easier, if you've got a lot of work to do and there's a happy atmosphere to do it in.

We are all part of history aren't we, in a very minor way, each one of us? I saw the Silver Jubilee of King George V and Queen Mary when I was in London, and I did see the funeral of King George V. It's all part of history, and especially living through the war.

Having the radio too, that brought it home to us. You could keep up to date. We thoroughly enjoyed our radio, in the kitchen. It wasn't quite like the television, but you were aware of things and if you'd got any imagination at all, you could imagine things that were going on in the world. We used to have the music on and we used to sing 'Auf Wiedersehen' and 'In the Chapel in the Moonlight'. They were the loveliest songs – and a lot more tune to them than what there is today.

I didn't ever think about coming to Blickling, nor about being a cook at that time. I didn't think I was experienced enough. But I came to Blickling, settled in here nicely, found a young man – and that was that! I was friends with my husband and he wanted us to get married. I wasn't really sure about getting married. I would have liked to have gone in the forces but he wasn't very keen about that. He thought I would meet somebody else! I couldn't have wished for a better husband. He had a lot to put up with!

After Blickling I went to the Bethel Hospital and worked in the kitchen there, which was a different experience altogether. We had to cook for the patients and for the nurses and staff as well. There were two of us cooks there and a kitchen maid, and a woman in the scullery as well, for washing-up. I wasn't there very long.

My other joy in life is sewing. I always loved it – and helped my mother. So I went to work at Harmer's making uniforms for air crew. I got on very well there, and that's what I did in the wartime until I found out I was expecting. When I went to Harmer's the girls there laughed at me – 'skivvying' they called it. But the people I met in service were streets above them. For a long time afterwards I wouldn't tell people I'd been in service. You wouldn't say anything about it. But now people are interested because it's a way of life that has almost gone.

I met my future husband Robert Wadlow at a dance. There was going to be a dance at Heydon village hall for the Poppy Appeal and we all cycled over there. We used to put our hair in curlers and put our dresses in an attaché case on the back of our bikes, and we took our curlers out when we got to the village hall, and put our dresses on – all dressed up like a dog's dinner. My husband was there; he was rather a shy young man. He always was rather shy, but I thought how nice he was – and he had lovely auburn hair. I teased him rather a lot – that's how we became friends. He worked at the lime kiln at Heydon.

I married in March 1940 and I should imagine I was the only girl ever to get married from the Bethel Hospital. I walked from the hospital down to St Peter Mancroft. I found a little house in Norwich and gave up my job and went to live there.

Bob was in the Territorials and was posted to Weybourne and Cheshire, before going abroad with the Royal Norfolks to Singapore, in 1941. I didn't really know whether he was alive or dead for ages. He didn't know when Terry was born – not for a long time, and Terry never saw his father until he was nearly four.

We had the Blitz in Norwich and my mother-in-law,

who lived in Corpusty, said, 'You don't want to stay up here in Norwich and get killed, with a baby coming as well.' She knew where there was a little cottage in Heydon – part of a wood it was. Would I like to go there? She said, 'Should I go and ask the lady, Mrs Bulwer [Senior] if you can have that?' My mother-in-law told her I'd been a cook at Blickling, so they knew about me and they said I could have that cottage. While I was staying with my mother-in-law, they put a new roof on the cottage and they put me a new copper in the kitchen for my washing and an oven in the wall. That was lovely and oh, that cooked lovely bread and pastry. Of course there was no electricity or anything there – just this little cottage. I had a well in the garden and had to draw all the water, and had to use that and boil a copper for washing. That was everyday work for mothers with children in them days – all that rubbing on a washboard. Although I soon had my baby, and it was lovely to look after him, that was really the saddest part of my life, hearing nothing from my husband.

Mrs Bulwer wrote to me once and put 'Bluestone Hall' as the address. My Uncle Alf [who was the

Charter Mayor of Dagenham] was thrilled at that, so he drew me a coat of arms. It had a well, an axe to chop the wood with and a blackcurrant tart to go in the oven in the wall!

'Bluestone Hall' was the rather grand name for this cottage near Heydon, where Flo lived after her marriage.

I hadn't been in Heydon all that long when Mrs Bulwer came and said she'd heard that I'd been a cook, and her cook had left, so would I go and cook her lunch at The Grange? At first it was just lunches. There was rationing, so we couldn't have too great meals, but I noticed that she always managed a bit better than some people. Well of course, it was understandable, because living on an estate, the farm had pigs and there were chickens. Before the war days and after the war, Heydon Hall was lived in by the Bulwer family, but it was let to people during the war.

Mrs Bulwer ('Aunt Bee' to the family) was a marvellous person. She was a very autocratic old lady, but that didn't cut any ice with me! We got on ever so well really and she was very kind. She had a lot to do with the Friends of Norwich Castle. Her collection of teapots is there. She had a whole room at The Grange, with shelves and teapots. To start with I just went about three mornings a week and cooked a meal. My little boy Terry was just about one when I went to cook for her and he used to come too. When he toddled about he could play outside and the gardener, Mr Rowe (who was the chauffeur as well), would take him for a ride in a barrow, on a pile of garden rubbish! Terry thoroughly enjoyed it as well.

Mrs Bulwer did have a maid, Alice, who was her personal maid and housemaid. Once, Alice went home for her holiday and Mrs Bulwer asked me if I'd come and live in for a while. She used to invite me into the drawing room after she had had her supper at night, so we could listen to the nine o'clock news on the wireless and hear how the war was going on.

My cousin had been in the Merchant Navy and was going to get married. They lived at Chadwell Heath, near Romford, and I was invited to go to the wedding. Mrs Bulwer said, 'Oh you must go.' But I said, 'The war has just finished and people are beginning to hear about the prisoners coming home.' So she said, 'I'll go and see the postmistress and if there's a telegram for you, they can bring it to me and I will ring your uncle up, where you're staying, and make sure you get the news.' And I got the news on the day of my cousin's wedding. That was the day when I heard my husband was alive and would be coming home.

On the Monday after the wedding, me and Terry came home by train, to Cawston. Mrs Bulwer with her car and chauffeur came to meet us at the station. She brought the telegram as well, and took me back to Heydon.

The Bulwer family asked me one day whether I would like to come and live in the village, and I said, 'As long as there's electric light!' And they said 'yes'.

'I'll come!' I replied. I never looked at the cottage or anything. So I was actually in the village by the time my husband arrived home, nearly a month later. He came home by boat, and it was a good thing in a way, 'cause they could build them up. They were like skeletons. Later I moved over the road, next to the smithy, and lived in this cottage for almost fifty years.

After my husband came home, I left Mrs Bulwer and later on I had my other son, Rob. The Bulwer family asked my husband if he'd like a job on Heydon estate – which he took. After a time Mrs Bulwer left The Grange and went and lived in 'The Old Cottage' [featured in the film *The Go-Between*].

Mrs Mary Bulwer, her niece, had married the gentleman who was to become Brigadier Long. Later her maiden name was added and she became Mrs Bulwer-Long, to preserve the Norfolk 'Bulwer' name. With her husband in the army they were out in Germany for a long time after the war.

But they nearly always used to come home in the school holidays, to The Grange in Heydon. One time

Mrs Bulwer-Long came and asked me if I would go and do the cooking while they were there, which I did. For Mrs Bulwer-Long I did a lot of other things and a lot of her friends would ask me to go and do dinner parties, or lunch parties.

The Brigadier came out of the army and he came home, so I used to go in more regularly. While the children were growing up they used to let the Hall to different people and often I would do dinner parties for them.

I enjoyed, and still enjoy cooking – any kind really, whether it's making ordinary cakes or wedding cakes, cooking a meal or doing a buffet. I've done no end of things since I left full-time service. I went to the Tech, but through the WI I did a special icing course. Then, when Miss Mary Anne Long got married [to Mr Charles Shippam] at Heydon, I made their wedding cake. I also made her going-away outfit! And of course – all the girls in the village – I made *their* wedding cakes, and for a lot of them I made wedding dresses or bridesmaids' dresses. When Captain William Bulwer-Long got married to Miss Sarah Rawlinson [daughter of Sir Frederick Rawlinson] it was at St Margaret's in Westminster. Of course we had a coach, and all the village went up for that. I made the cake, which was taken up to London for the reception in the Hyde Park Hotel. I was very proud when the head waiter asked Lady Rawlinson, 'Is the lady here who made the cake?'

'Oh yes,' she replied, 'Mrs Wadlow's here.' He asked if he could be introduced to me and he said it was one of the nicest cakes he'd ever cut.

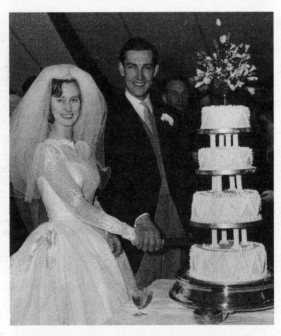

The cake made by Flo for the wedding of
Mary Anne (née Long) and Charles Shippam

Flo became involved in the life of the parish church of St Peter and St Paul during her time in Heydon, taking her share of the usual village duties of Parochial Church Council membership and through this, representing the village on the deanery synod. Flo took her turn with the flower arranging and with reading the lessons, and even made three altar frontals in white, green and red.

Flo's interests have been many, the WI and the Red Cross particularly.

'Costume through the ages' being portrayed by the ladies of Heydon WI, photographed outside 'The Old Cottage'. Mrs Bulwer ('Aunt Bee') is seated far right, with Flo standing beside her.

I was always interested in the WI and that really enhanced my life quite a lot. It didn't matter what craft you name – we had lessons in it. Mrs Bulwer-Long [the younger] was to do with the Red Cross, and we were in the Red Cross. I've got my medals now. Once a year we used to have a big Red Cross Ball, which Mrs Bulwer-Long and I catered for.

Another memorable Red Cross event for Flo was taking part in the Guard of Honour for the Queen outside Sandringham House, composed of representatives of eighty-five Norfolk detachments. On that occasion the Queen named the first mobile hospital unit of the County British Red Cross, with Lady Walpole, the County President, accompanying Her Majesty.

A splendid Red Cross event with a big surprise for Flo and a Red Cross colleague was the fashion show presented at Blickling Hall on October 1st 1960, featuring British fashion house Lachasse. The local paper reported:

The two ladies have done a good deal of helping behind the scenes at big events and last Saturday they went along to the big fashion show at

Blickling Hall to give, they thought, some more of the same kind of help. Instead they found themselves at the very centre of everything – helping to dress the models. They are both keen dressmakers . . . and they had a wonderful opportunity to see these marvellous creations and their fabrics at the closest quarters.

Flo (far right) helping out with the teas

And Flo always rose to the challenge of catering, it would seem, whatever the event.

When Mrs Bulwer-Long was the head of the Norfolk Pony Club, they used to have their camp in Heydon

Park, and they would have a special day when they jumped for the cups. We would give lunch to all the judges. They would come in when they were ready, because they were judging different events. Then we had Mr Gordon Parker, the founder of the Felixstowe Docks. I always used to do their shooting-party lunches. For his seventieth birthday he had about two hundred people there that night. And that was the night of the Royal Norfolk Show. It wasn't a big meal; they had drinks and they had a lot of canapés, and I made a big birthday cake. I had a big oven that you roast your meat in and I made the cake in that. Mr Parker's daughter said, 'Oh Mrs Wadlow, I hope we don't have any left.' But it was gone – just like that. There wasn't a bit left.

Flo's interest in drama started at school, so it is of little surprise to have found her as a regular member of the 'Heydon Minstrels'. This local village group was set up at the instigation of one of the American tenants at the Hall, Sergeant Dextras, and it provided a wide range of entertainment over a number of years, including pantomimes and Old Time Music Hall.

The 'Heydon Minstrels'

Flo also took part in the WI Pageant, 'Kett's Rebellion', at the Royal Norfolk showground in 1982.

WI pageant, 'Kett's Rebellion'

Flo's considerable skills as a needlewoman were put to very good use over the years. Flo designed a tapestry chair for Heydon Hall and hassocks for Norwich Cathedral. When in the early 1970s an appeal was made for volunteer workers to create hassocks for the Chapel of the Most Excellent Order of the British Empire, in St Paul's Cathedral, Flo responded. Her heart sank somewhat when the complicated patterns arrived, but never turning down a challenge, Flo set about creating her hassock, and then volunteered for another. The service of dedication was held in the Cathedral on 22nd November 1972.

Three years later, in 1975, Flo repeated the work, this time for the Regimental Memorial for the Middlesex Regiment, again in St Paul's. Colonel Clayton, the President of the Association, wrote thanking Flo:

I am writing on behalf of the Middlesex Regiment and its Association to thank you very much indeed for your help in making those beautiful hassocks for use in the Regimental Chapel in St Paul's Cathedral. It is really most kind of you to have given up your time to do this and I can assure you that your invaluable and unselfish help is much appreciated.

It was especially appreciated by the family of the soldier to whom one of Flo's hassocks was dedicated:

Dear Mrs Wadlow,

In the course of a recent letter from my sister, Mrs Phelps, she gives me a glowing account of a really handsome and skilfully made kneeler which you have recently completed for the Middlesex Regimental Memorial in St Paul's Cathedral, in which you have incorporated not only the regimental crest, but also my father's initials and dates in his special memory.

I feel I must write and thank you for this work. I do not know if any of the other kneelers being made are so personal i.e. bearing the initials of individuals, but I doubt it. The one you have made will therefore have a special significance for all who see it, and particularly for members of my family. I hope that my children and grandchildren, visiting St Paul's in future years, will find this kneeler and be proud to think 'That was our ancestor, especially worked in his memory by the lady who worked it.' Needless to say, I shall be proud of it myself, and I look forward to seeing it on a future visit to the Cathedral.

Yours truly,

Duncan Stewart

Flo's husband was associated with the Far East Prisoners of War Association, and although he sadly died in 1983, Flo continued the connection. In 1992 – and by a remarkable coincidence, on 8th December, the exact day of her eightieth birthday – Flo was invited to a reception in London's Guildhall, for the National Federation of Far East Prisoners of War Clubs and Associations. It was a glittering occasion in the presence of the Queen Mother. Flo shook the hand of the Queen Mother and the Lord Mayor of London. She spoke to the ceremonial pikemen and met Dame Vera Lynn as she was leaving the Guildhall. A splendid eightieth birthday present!

July 14th 1998 was also a very special day for Flo, when she attended a Buckingham Palace Garden Party accompanied by her granddaughter, Paula. Flo believes her name was put forward because of her very long membership of the WI.

Our day started early with a trip to the hairdresser's at 7.40 a.m., then home to have a chat with Radio Norfolk, who wished us a happy day. Time to don our finery and out with our cameras to record our looks, then off to Norwich to board the train for London. On the platform we were greeted by a lady, 'I know where you're going.' A British Legion member, she also had an invitation. In London we travelled by Underground to St James's Park, a short walk from the Palace. Of course there were hundreds of people queuing to enter. It was fascinating to study the various fashions – long skirts and mini ones, flowery and plain dresses, all in a variety of colours and styles. The *hats*! Large ones plumed with feathers, straw ones garlanded with flowers and others a froth of veiling and ribbons. What a gala day for milliners. They must bless the Queen for ordering hats to be worn.

Slowly the queues moved forward through the gates, across the courtyard and up the red-carpeted stairs; at last we were in the Palace – what splendour. Ushered through a couple of rooms and out into the garden, more like a park really. Sun shining, band playing, tea tent beckoning with a tasty array of dainty sandwiches and cakes.

The Yeomen of the Guard, resplendent in their red-and-gold uniforms, lined up, down the steps and across the lawn, to form a path for the Queen and

Duke to walk through the crowds of guests. The Queen was dressed in a royal-blue silk coat and hat to match, with a flowery dress. We sat near the entrance to the Royal Tea Tent so had a very good view of Her Majesty as she went into tea, but not near enough to say hello.

A Gentleman of the Queen's Household on duty in the Royal enclosure asked Paula about her badge and she told him it was a Norfolk Women's Institute one. He replied, 'How nice to meet a young member.' I told him how proud and honoured we felt to be fellow members with the Queen and Queen Mother. All too soon it was time to go, and what a day. The magic lingers on.

EⅡR

*The Lord Chamberlain is
commanded by Her Majesty to invite*

Mrs. Wilfred Wadlow

*to a Garden Party
at Buckingham Palace
on Tuesday 14th July 1998 from 4 to 6 pm*

This card does not admit

Sharing the memories of her life in service has led to a mini media career for Flo. She featured in a press interview with Gillian Shephard no less, who was then researching at the UEA into domestic service in grand houses. She was interviewed by that indefatigable Norfolk flag-flier, Keith Skipper, during his time working for Radio Norfolk, and contributed to the national radio series The Century Speaks, *in addition to her own programme,* Cooking Up a Royal Treat, *for BBC Radio 4, as mentioned above. On television she has been interviewed by Susie Fowler-Watt, and has also ventured into national television with the series* Upper Crust, *presented by author and photographer Christopher Simon Sykes. Here Flo starred with Mrs Sarah Bulwer-Long in the kitchen of one of Flo's favourite houses, Heydon Hall. As at Blickling, she made the 'Royal' chicken dish. Flo commented:*

The film crew were most intrigued by my experiences and told me I was a natural for television! I'm not a person who's a bit shy and, with cooking, I don't get worried if anyone looks at me. Why would I? It's been my life.

I've given my talk about my life in service to ever so many WIs, and lots of organisations in the Fakenham area and around the county, and nearly every time they've said, 'You ought to write a book!'

When some years ago the National Trust at Blickling produced a children's guidebook, 'Mrs Wadlow' featured in it, to help the children find their way around.

Mrs Wadlow in the Blickling children's guidebook

And when the National Trust wanted a speaker to address their members, Flo surprised them because she is never at a loss for words.

One time they asked me at Blickling Hall if I would go there and talk to a lot of the people who belong to the National Trust, so we had a whole group, all in the Hall. The man who was head of the National Trust at Blickling said he was absolutely amazed. He thought I would talk for about half an hour and then I'd run out of steam. He said, 'There you are, more than an hour later, still going!'

Flo in the kitchen of Heydon Hall during
the filming of *Upper Crust* in 1998

EPILOGUE

Florence Wadlow died on 9th January 2013, at the age of 100. The *Daily Telegraph* paid tribute to her with a detailed obituary. Flo was unimpressed by the TV programmes *Upstairs, Downstairs* and *Downton Abbey*, saying: 'They have got it wrong. They should have talked to people like me.'

APPENDIX

Recipes

Just as most of the horsemen had their books of remedies handed down from generation to generation, closely guarded secrets that were said to earn a man a living, so most cooks, even if they will not admit to them, usually have, secreted away, a little notebook of recipes. These are often the distillation of a lifetime's cooking, the firm favourites that have found their place of honour on the handwritten pages. Flo of course had such a book, and was prepared to share one or two of its secrets . . .

The Famous (almost a disaster) Blickling Ginger Sponge

Ingredients: 7 ozs flour, 1 heaped tsp baking powder, 4 ozs butter, 5 ozs sugar, 3 eggs, ½ teacup of milk, 1 heaped tsp ground ginger

Method: Cream butter and sugar, add eggs and beat well. Sift flour, ginger and baking powder. Add milk. Bake in moderate oven for about 50 minutes.

Mexican Gateau

Ingredients: ¾ lb self-raising flour, ¾ lb sugar, 6 ozs butter, 4 eggs, 2 oranges, 2 ozs shelled Brazil nuts

Method: Peel one orange thinly and cut peel into very fine strips. Chop nuts. Cream butter and sugar, add well-beaten eggs and the juice of 1 ½ oranges, add other ingredients. Bake in sandwich tin, in moderate oven, testing after 30 minutes. Put together with filling.

Marmalade Cake

Ingredients: 1 lb flour, 6 ozs fat (marg./lard), 6 ozs caster sugar, 6 ozs mixed currants and sultanas, 2 tbsp marmalade, 1 tsp bicarb., milk

Method: Rub fat in flour. Add sugar, currants, sultanas and marmalade. Dissolve bicarb. in warm water and add to milk. Bake in moderate oven and test after 40–45 minutes.

Mrs Aves' Church Warden's Cake

Ingredients: 1 cup soft brown sugar (6 ozs), 1 lb mixed fruit, 6 ozs marg., 1 tsp bicarb., 1 cup cold water, small tin condensed milk, ½ lb chopped dates, ¼ lb cherries, 2 ozs chopped walnuts, 1 ½ cups self-raising flour, 2 beaten eggs

Method: Bring to boil all ingredients (except flour and eggs), and simmer for 20 mins. Leave to cool. Stir in flour and eggs. Cook in 7- or 8-inch tin at 325 degrees for 1 ¼ to 1 ½ hours.

Rainbow Cake

Ingredients: 6 ozs marg. or butter, 6 ozs sugar (caster or gran.), 3 eggs, 6 ozs self-raising flour, 1 dsp cocoa, 1 dsp of pink blancmange powder – either strawberry or raspberry (if you cannot get blancmange powder, use 'Angel Delight'), green colouring

Method: Beat marg. and sugar together then stir in eggs and flour. If you have an electric mixer this can be done all at once. Divide the mixture into 4 basins. In one add cocoa, add strawberry to another basin, add drops of green colour to the next and leave one plain. From each basin put different spoonfuls of colour into two 8-inch greased sponge tins, and bake at 350 degrees. Test after 30–40 minutes.